DATE DUE

HIRING THE RIGHT PERSON FOR THE RIGHT JOB

SKILLS FOR SUCCESS

LEADERSHIP:
The Key to Management Success
by L. Bittel

MANAGING YOURSELF:
How to Control Emotion, Stress, and Time
by A. Goodloe, J. Bensahel, and J. Kelly

COMMUNICATING:
How to Organize Meetings and Presentations
by J. Callanan

HIRING THE RIGHT PERSON FOR THE RIGHT JOB
by C. Dobrish, R. Wolff, and B. Zevnik

MORALE AND MOTIVATION:
How to Measure Morale and Increase Productivity
by E. Benge and J. Hickey

CECELIA DOBRISH
RICK WOLFF
BRIAN ZEVNIK

HIRING THE RIGHT PERSON FOR THE RIGHT JOB

A GROLIER COMPANY

FRANKLIN WATTS

New York   London   Toronto   Sydney

Library of Congress Cataloging in Publication Data

Dobrish, Cecelia.
  Hiring the right person for the right job.

  Includes index.
  1. Recruiting of employees.   I. Wolff, Rick, 1951–
II. Zevnik, Brian.   III. Title.
HF5549.5.R44D63   1984   658.3'11   84-11927
ISBN 0-531-09576-2

CONTENTS

EXHIBITS

INTRODUCTION

As every smart manager knows, a company is only as good
as its people. . . .

- It makes little difference how great your product is—
  you still need good, solid employees to market it.

- Your firm's technology may be more advanced than
  anybody else's. But unless your technicians are well
  trained and loyal, your state-of-the-art technology won't
  go anywhere.

- Your on-line workers may come up with some brilliant
  ideas regarding production. But unless your supervisors
  know enough to listen to their subordinates, those great
  ideas will never materialize.

What's the point of all these illustrations? Simple. It
doesn't really matter how great your product is, or your
company is, or even the CEO—without a sturdy framework

of capable, reliable employees, your company will never prosper. That's why this book was put together. It starts at the absolute beginning of a company's needs in terms of personnel, and builds, step by step, into a perfect guide to what you need to know to hire the best people.

The first section deals with job descriptions. Before you can determine who's the best candidate for the job, you have to first pinpoint just what that job is and what kind of credentials are needed for it. You might be surprised at just how difficult that kind of project can be, but you'll find in this section all kinds of sample job descriptions, from clerical positions to upper-level management.

After you've mastered the art of writing a job description, your next step is to get the word out—to let people know that you're interested in hiring the right personnel. Most people know about the classified advertising in newspapers, but there are several proven methods of finding topflight people that many managers aren't aware of. You'll read about some of these techniques in the chapters focusing on employee recruitment.

From there, you'll have to put together a standard application form for job candidates. With today's intricate Equal Employment Opportunity (EEO) laws, every employer has to know just what can—and cannot—be asked of a job applicant. Here again, you'll find precise definitions of what is legal these days; also a sample standard application form that you can copy and an easy-to-read checklist of EEO laws regarding application forms.

The second section of the book examines the current state of employee testing. Since employee tests are objective in nature and have a well-established track record of reliability in pinpointing employee strengths and weaknesses, more and more companies are utilizing them.

The problem is that there are literally hundreds of business tests, ranging from computer skills to manual dexterity to reading comprehension. You'll find all the answers to your questions about employee testing in this section, plus plenty of listings of where you can find out more about these exams. And as above, there's a review of EEO considerations regarding employee testing.

Finally, you've put together a list of the best-qualified candidates for that job opening, and you've decided to interview each and every one of them. This is your opportunity to see all of the job applicants in person.

But interviewing any job applicant these days is a lot more complicated than it was, say, twenty years ago. On one hand, you want to extract as much vital information and data as you can from the individual and do so in a friendly and diplomatic way. On the other hand, with all the federal regulations regarding interviewing procedures, you have to walk a careful path so as not to ask questions that are patently illegal.

The last section of this book centers on just this difficult process. By following the suggestions, hints, cues, and guidelines put forth, you'll be able to make the most out of these interviews—and in the end, feel fully confident that you have found the very best candidate for that job.

PART I

HOW TO DEVELOP A JOB DESCRIPTION PROGRAM

DEVELOPMENT
OF A JOB DESCRIPTION
PROGRAM

Steps that need to be taken before embarking on a major program for developing and writing job descriptions include: determining the organization's needs, ensuring cooperation from top-level management, and selecting an administrator.

DETERMINING THE ORGANIZATION'S NEEDS

A number of symptoms usually lead management to consider starting a job description program:

Pay practices are inadequate and lack consistency.

Employees complain that they do not know what specific work is required of them; frequent conflicts and misunderstandings occur.

Supervisors overlap responsibility and authority, leading to duplication of effort and occasional conflict.

Hiring and selection is ineffective; people are assigned to work for which they are not qualified.

The work force is not adequately trained.

The organization's overall productivity is not acceptable to management.

The flow of work is not smooth; it suffers delays and is incomplete.

A well-planned and executed job description program helps fill management's needs in key personnel areas such as compensation, hiring and selection, organizational design, performance appraisal and manpower planning. These needs are continuing and so should the program to satisfy them. Such a system should not be started simply to fulfill a one-time objective.

Evaluating Costs Against Benefits

Job descriptions do not provide the only cure for these symptoms. They may be the result of improper supervisory practices, undesirable workplace conditions or other causes. Before management commits the sizable human resources required by a comprehensive job description program, it should determine whether the program will adequately cure the symptoms mentioned.

In calculating the costs, management should recognize that the program, once started, must be maintained. It requires constant updating. If continuing top-management commitment is not possible, then the program should be installed only at the levels where its maintenance can be conveniently managed.

Ensuring Cooperation

To ensure the success of a job description program, the support of top management must be visible. Top executives must communicate their desires for the program and what they expect of lower-level managers and supervisors. The more widespread the participation among managers and supervisors in the program's development, the more important this communication becomes. The company president or other top executive responsible for job descriptions should issue a formal notice, a policy statement to those persons who will certainly be involved. Exhibit 1 shows a typical example of such a communication. It includes these key elements:

The primary purpose for establishing a job description program.

The person or group who will be responsible for its development and implementation.

The organizational units covered by the program.

An outline of the schedule for implementation.

The procedure for review of the drafts of descriptions.

What will be required of employees and managers in developing the program.

It is critical to create a climate of cooperation and positive participation by all persons involved. Whether a company undertakes a comprehensive job description program in which every employee is eventually a participant—or a more limited effort—disinterest and distrust must be dispelled before the program begins. Some methods for obtaining maximum cooperation are:

EXHIBIT 1

Memorandum Introducing a Job Description Program

TO: All Managers and Supervisors

In an effort to establish a fair and equitable compensation system for all our employees, we have determined that a formal Wage and Salary Plan needs to be instituted in the course of this year.

As a first step we have appointed a committee of three people to develop and initiate a job description program throughout the organization.

The committee members are Mr. S. Simpson, Miss R. Holmes and Mr. F. McDonald, who will also act as coordinator of the committee. Mr. B. Thomas, personnel manager, will serve on the committee ex-officio.

We have charged the committee with the responsibility to initiate the necessary effort through the Personnel Department to oversee the program and to review all draft descriptions for consistency prior to their approval by general management. We expect this work to be completed by year-end.

Members of the Personnel Department will meet with you individually or in small groups to acquaint you with the details of the program, as well as the general schedules.

Your participation in this program is a necessary ingredient for its completion. You will be requested by the committee to assist in drafting initial descriptions of the jobs for which you hold responsibility. Therefore your full cooperation will be significant in making the program successful.

H. J. Harding
President

Delegating to one manager the responsibility for communicating program details to operating supervisors.

Undertaking a pilot program with a small organizational unit to detect and correct any deficiencies. This should be done after the policy statement has been issued.

Holding preliminary meetings with managers and supervisors to answer questions, uncover conflicts, clarify goals and evaluate suggestions from participants.

SELECTING A PROGRAM ADMINISTRATOR

The program administrator establishes procedures, develops formats, directs the gathering of information, monitors progress, and sees to it that the program stays on schedule. His or her most important responsibilities involve eliminating overlaps in descriptions, making sure that descriptions are written in a uniform style, administering the review, revision and approval procedures, and making sure that the drafts of the descriptions become final.

Thus, the person appointed as program administrator must be familiar with the company, its work units and functional divisions. He or she must be respected by everyone from top managers to line supervisors. The program administrator and line supervisors should have a common purpose: mutual confidence and trust.

Some companies use an outside consultant to introduce a new job description program. Such consultants are used to varying degrees, which sometimes include total responsibility for preparing the final company manual of job descriptions. Some companies engage the consultant to act as advisor to the administrator. Such an individual may lend direction, share experiences, suggest methods or provide critical services that the company lacks. His or her role is to enhance the expertise of the program's administrator while the program takes shape.

EEO Insight—What's wrong with this job description?

Take a look at the following job description that was written by a personnel manager at a publishing house. See if you notice any inherent problems with the way it's written:

> TITLE: Editorial Assistant
>
> Involved with all aspects of editorial production, from acquisition of manuscripts to final bound volume. Position really has no sharply defined duties, but calls for a real "Gal Friday" type.
>
> Individual reports to both editor in chief and production manager.
>
> GENERAL DUTIES: Broad contact with authors, doing rewrites, editing, proofreading, publicity, and marketing ideas.
>
> QUALIFICATIONS: Must be recent college graduate, be able to type 50 wpm, and have no problem in working long hours.

The problems you should have spotted:

1. First, as you'll see in the next chapter, this entire job description is much too brief and sketchy. There is no really explicit explanation of what this job entails; just to write "involved with all aspects of editorial production" does not help an individual understand what is involved.

2. Under Equal Employment Opportunity laws, specifying a "Gal Friday" type is immediately discriminatory against men who might be interested in the position. Be wary of such sexist remarks in your job decriptions. They may mean no harm, but such statements wave a red flag and should be avoided.

3. "Must be recent college graduate" can also be interpreted by the EEO as age discrimination. There's an implication here that one must be in one's early twenties in order to be fit for the job. These days, when age discrimination lawsuits are on the rise, be particularly careful with such descriptions.

4. Reports to two bosses. There's an old saying about how difficult it is for somebody to have to serve two masters. That saying may be old, but it's still true today. Real problems can occur when an individual subordinate has to report to two separate and distinct bosses.

5. The general impression you get from reading such a job description is that the position must experience a great deal of employee turnover and, judging from the work involved, it's certainly understandable why. Not only are there problems with the EEO requirements, but the job itself seems poorly defined and understood.

2

TYPES OF
JOB DESCRIPTIONS

Job descriptions share certain common characteristics, though they can be written in different ways. A job description is a concise document of factual information that identifies the work to be performed and the responsibility entailed in a job. It outlines relationships between the job and other jobs in the organization, the requirements for performing the work and its frequency or scope. The description is based upon the nature of the work rather than on the individual currently performing it.

TWO KINDS OF JOB DESCRIPTIONS

Generic descriptions are written in broadly stated terms without identifying specific tasks and responsibilities. They provide a comprehensive overview of a job category by means of the common denominators of all jobs that fall within a category. To write a generic description, a number of jobs must be analyzed to find their common denominators.

For example, a generic description of "Senior Accountant" includes the area of expertise expected of that professional level. It does not cover the specific functions— accounts payable or receivable, general ledger specialty— or the smaller organizational unit within the accounting department to which the job reports. Exhibit 2 gives an example of a generic job description.

The generic form is generally used for the following:

• Development of training programs

• Recruiting

• Organizational planning

• Development of performance standards

• Manpower planning

• Salary surveys

Specific job descriptions provide the precise duties and tasks of a job. They show its relationships with other specific jobs within the smallest organizational units.

For example, the specific job "General Ledger Accountant" should identify the job's reporting relationships within the accounting department. It will show the type of accounting systems used, the nature and frequency of financial reports to be prepared, and the limits of responsibility within geographic, functional or other parts of the company.

Exhibit 3 shows a specific job description. It is an actual description used by several companies. It contains some

EXHIBIT 2

A Generic Job Description

Title: Management Systems Analyst

Charter:
As used here, "systems" refers to the logical overall approach or method used for the orderly means of data collection, processing and production of useful information, the objective of which is to improve control and decision making through the efficient use of data processing equipment.

Work Performed:
Analyzes and develops well-scoped subsystems generally involving a single or similar functional area of corporate and divisional operations.

Works with "user" personnel determining their detailed requirements and procedures, developing detailed instructions for conversion and system operations; trains "users" in proper use of the system.

With supervision, assumes responsibility for development of well-scoped and semidefined subsystems, including basic forms design, manual preparation, programming specifications, and detailed systems documentation.

Evaluates cost differentials with system implementation against varying contingencies.

Areas of Application:
Primarily found in data processing organization or management systems organization and sometimes in the high-volume user organization.

Qualifications:
Normally a four-year bachelor's degree from an accredited institution with two or more years of experience, OR a master's degree.

EXHIBIT 3

Sample of a Specific Job Description—Corporate Controller

Position Description

CORPORATE CONTROLLER

Reports to: Treasurer

Supervises: Assigned Staff

Basic Function:

The corporate controller is responsible for the direction and coordination of the accounting activities of the company, including development, maintenance, preparation, and interpretation of corporate accounting records, financial reports, statistics, accounting policies and procedures, government reports, and office and data processing services.

Primary Duties and Responsibilities:

1. Develops and implements plans and objectives for the department.

2. Develops for approval and implements accounting standards and procedures to assure uniform accounting practices, adequate internal controls, and compliance with orders or regulations issued by government agencies.

   • Applies modern internal control principles and techniques in the development of accounting methods and control reports.

   • Issues all procedures defining the manner in which financial accounting transactions are to be recorded and reported.

   • Maintains surveillance over the accounting systems employed in the company and initiates changes as necessary.

(continued)

3. Directs and controls preparation and maintenance of corporate financial, accounting, and statistical records, including general accounting and property accounting.

4. Provides functional direction, coordination, and advice to area administration managers in their accounting activities:

   - Cost accounting
   - General accounting
   - Billing procedures
   - General office management

5. Directs and controls payroll and other general office activities for the corporate staff, including supervision of the data processing center.

6. Counsels with corporate department heads, area general managers, and others in operating management on accounting matters and on interpretation and use of related reports.

7. Develops and recommends the organization structure and staffing, compensation, hiring, termination, transfer, and promotion of all personnel under his or her direction.

Principal Working Relationships:
(Excluding direct reporting relationships)

1. Works with the assistant treasurer to coordinate accounting policies and operations with cash management, billing, revenue, insurance, and real estate operations.

2. Works with the systems and procedures manager to coordinate accounting and management information systems and to provide data processing services.

3. Works with the budgeting manager to coordinate the requirements of budgeting and accounting systems.

4. Works with area general managers and administration managers to provide accounting systems and to provide advice and assistance in accounting activities.

variances from the consensus illustrated in Exhibit 4. But that is to be expected when obtaining information from different sources who have their individual opinions about the presentation of job descriptions. The specific job description type serves other purposes:

* Precise job analysis

* Job evaluation (for wage and salary administration)

* Table of organization

HOW TO CHOOSE
THE TYPE OF JOB
DESCRIPTION TO WRITE

An important factor determining whether to write a generic or specific job description is the resources that are required to keep descriptions current. A viable program requires continual revision and updating. The detail required to write and keep specific job descriptions up-to-date sometimes tempts program administrators to generalize descriptions into generic forms. However, filling the descriptions with ambiguities or allowing them to show overlapping responsibilities defeats the purpose of the program.

Formats of Job Descriptions

There is a consensus among experts on style, content, and form for job descriptions. Exhibit 4 shows a format that can be adapted to suit any company initiating a job description program. This format helps identify a job description's critical characteristics and includes:

- *Job Title, Organizational Unit, and Accountability.* These items identify the job and give it its own unique characteristics. They make each job different from any other. Consequently, even two job descriptions with the same title and the same level of pay may have different duties, responsibilities, accountabilities or relationships. For example, the job of "designer" in the consumer products division and the industrial products division of the same manufacturing company might have the same level of pay, but differ markedly in other ways.

- *Job Summary, Duties and Responsibilities.* These define the work to be performed and provide the essential elements for subsequent analysis (as will be shown later in this manual).

- *Duties and Responsibilities.* This part of the job description describes "what" task is performed, "why" it is performed and, when it is not self-evident, "how" it is performed. If the *what*, *why* or the *how* is missing, the statement is incomplete.

- *Interaction.* Specifies the relationships between one job and another. When occupations are closely associated, the description of each job's interaction becomes critical. It is also important for describing jobs that have extensive relationships outside the company, for instance, sales, marketing and public relations jobs.

- *Prepared by, Approved by and Date.* Each description must show who has prepared it and whether it has received final approval or is merely in the draft stage. The identity of the writer, administrator or job analyst must be available should questions arise in the future. The date of preparation tells anyone reading it how current the information is.

REFINING THE LANGUAGE
USED IN THE DESCRIPTIONS

Take, for example, the two statements below giving the duties and responsibilities of the shift supervisor in a processing operation:

Insufficient:		Inspects operating equipment.
Complete:	(What)	Inspects equipment on a daily basis
	(Why)	to determine need for repair work
	(How)	through visual inspection and results of quality tests of the end products of the process.

The second statement clearly describes the shift supervisor's responsibility. It establishes the fact that the duties are to be performed on a daily basis, and states their exact purpose: to determine the need for repair (as contrasted to, say, cleanliness). Describing how the responsibility is carried out prevents ambiguity about the way the job is done. The statement reveals management's expectations for the job of shift supervisor.

In describing a job's "interaction" the writer makes sure that responsibilities among two or more descriptions do not overlap. The program administrator and operating managers when reviewing the drafts of job descriptions make certain that such duplications do not occur.

If, for instance, the description of marketing manager shows that one responsibility is "final approval for price

EXHIBIT 4

Typical Format of a Specific Job Description

NAME OF ORGANIZATION, COMPANY OR INSTITUTION

Job Title:

Organizational Unit: (Division, department, location, section, etc.)

Accountability:

(Title of person to which this job reports.)

Job Summary:

(A short statement outlining the purpose or "mission" of this job; its supervisory, technical or administrative scope and purview.)

Duties and Responsibilities:

(Series of statements, each outlining a particular duty, task, or responsibility and identifying "what," "why," and "how." All statements to be related to the work to be performed. Statements should identify the most predominant and significant duties and convey a measure of frequency of occurrence.)

Interaction:

(When significant to the job, a statement describing the relationships of the job with internal and external groups.)

Prepared By:

Approved By:

Date:

discounts," the same responsibility should not appear on the description of the sales representative or some other person. Similarly, if authority for extending customer credit rests with the financial manager, it should *not* also appear on the description of the marketing manager.

Relationships implied or assumed in the "interaction" section are also important. The description of the interaction depends on key statements made in "Job Summary, Duties and Responsibilities." For example, one statement in the duties and responsibilities section of a production engineer's description might read:

(What)   Reviews inspection reports and

(How)   analyzes causes of variance from quality standards to

(Why)   alert the production superintendent of potential loss of product due to rejection.

The "why" phrase defines one level of the production engineer's responsibility and also emphasizes the need for interaction between the engineer and the production superintendent.

There are many direct or implied interactions in most organizations. The job description should include those interactions most important to the performance of the job and clarify the interactions that are currently uncertain or that need to be redefined.

Key Skills, Requirements and Other Conditions of the Job

Job specifications are the requirements that applicants must meet if they are to be able to perform the duties, carry out the responsibilities and work smoothly with the persons to whom they report.

Although specifications are not, technically, part of a job description, key skills, requirements, and conditions are usually included somewhere. A qualifications section may be incorporated into the format as shown in Exhibit 2. Usually it is the minimum skill, experience, and knowledge needed to do the job that is included in the description rather than the skills or knowledge of persons who are now doing the job. Minimum requirements can include special job demands such as extensive travel or night hours in addition to the usual skill and experience requirements.

To avoid unrealistic requirements, job specifications should be based on how the work is being done currently. The following guide helps derive job specifications from current work practices:

Requirements related to individual doing the job	*Requirements related to working conditions*
Applicable education	Travel requirements
Applicable experience	Relocation requirements
Specific areas of expertise	Hours and schedules of work
Manual or mental skills	Hazardous or difficult environmental conditions
Interactive or social skills	

"JOB" VS. "POSITION"

The word "job" is often used interchangeably with "position." But there is a difference between the terms. *Position* refers to a particular assignment or appointment within the organizational framework. *Job* refers to an occupation consisting of a series of tasks that are grouped into a unit of work that can be performed by one person.

Three people could each have their own *positions* in a company, but perform the same *job*. For example, they could each have the position of shift supervisor on a different shift, but all perform the same job. Similarly, three people could each hold the position of computer programmer, but all do the same work at the same time in the same department.

Sometimes the two words denote differences in rank. A position description is generally used for higher-ranking managers, professionals and specialists. A job description is for lesser ranking technicians, clerks, and production and maintenance persons.

The practice of identifying higher-ranking assignments with position descriptions is an extension of the appointment/occupation distinction. Since management jobs can be held by only one person—such as president, sales manager, office manager—there is only one position for each job. Moreover, the content of a manager's job is likely to change with each appointee.

Each company can decide whether it wants to use a particular definition of position and job or to use them interchangeably. However, it is advisable to standardize the usage by using the term "job" for the occupation described and the term "position" for the individual's appointment or assignment.

JOB DESIGN

Usually companies start a job description program to describe existing practices: the current organizational framework, the present mode of operation. Sometimes, however, descriptions are used to restructure and change jobs. This process is called *job design* (or redesign).

Job design takes separate tasks and groups them into manageable units of work most suitable to meet various requirements such as staffing, work flow, supervision, training or control. It is often used to create a motivational climate among employees in a single department whose work has a common purpose or function.

Occasionally, the goal of job design is to adapt the job to the person doing it. This is done on a smaller scale— only one or two employees at a time.

There are three basic approaches to redesigning jobs:

1. *Enlarging* it horizontally by adding more tasks, or vertically by adding more responsibility.

2. *Diluting* it by removing tasks or taking away responsibilities.

3. *Restructuring* it by removing, adding or combining essential duties and responsibilities. Since job restructuring involves several jobs, it is really a form of reorganization.

Firms use job design for a variety of reasons:

To adapt jobs to changes in technology or other improvements in the state of the art.

To better utilize individual talents and expertise.

To improve organizational work flow.

To adapt tasks to take advantage of human resources outside the organization.

To create motivation in a job group by changing, reassigning and redirecting employees.

To reduce or expand the work force.

When jobs are redesigned, the program administrator and the operating managers are responsible for revising the descriptions of the jobs affected and for getting the revisions approved.

3

WRITING
JOB DESCRIPTIONS

In the previous chapter, Exhibit 4 gave a guide that writers of job descriptions can use to cover the parts of the description and the order in which these parts are best listed. The descriptions given in Exhibit 3 follow this guide generally, but not item by item. That is because these are actual job descriptions used by various companies. Not all preparers of descriptions follow exactly the guide this book suggests.

However, the first item logically should be the title of the job or position. An accurate job title has certain specific characteristics: it is self-evident, reflective of rank or worth, free of technical jargon and, as a rule, simple and recognizable. Duplication should be avoided.

There are two kinds of titles:

Generic titles name the central occupation or profession, showing rank, or level of expertise with qualifiers such as junior, senior, principal, first, second. Examples of generic titles are: electronics engineer, legal counsel, secretary, administrator.

Specific titles identify the particular role that a job plans in the organization. For example, computer design engineer, personnel secretary, administrator of contract compliance.

WHAT JOB TITLES SHOULD DO

A job title, whether generic or specific, should do the following:

> Name the occupation to be described in a way that is clear and recognizable to all employees. For example, computer programmer as contrasted to PDP-80 programmer.

> Be acceptable to employees and managers alike. For example, in a law office it is more acceptable to the employee to be known as legal secretary than as office secretary.

The United States Training and Employment Service of the Manpower Administration, U.S. Department of Labor, Washington, D.C., U.S.A., has compiled a *Dictionary of Occupational Titles*. It is a useful aid to title selection.

Organizational unit. The next part of the description, organizational unit, helps identify the job. It shows where the job is done: geographically, by division, by department. This information aids cataloging job description and is useful when the description is used for manpower planning, recruiting and other organizational purposes.

Accountability. In the specific job description given in Exhibit 3, accountability is described in terms of reporting relationships. This part of the description helps to clarify the place of the manufacturing manager in the organizational structure of the company.

Duties and responsibilities. Duties and responsibilities are given in clear, concise statements telling *what* the duty is, *how* it is performed, and *why* it is performed. Some elements may be left out to prevent repetition or to avoid stating the obvious. For example, the description need not clarify a phrase describing typing tasks by saying that the tasks are performed on a typewriter. But, where the method (how) and the reason (why) are different from what is implied, the writer should clarify it. For instance, a data processing programmer's task can be clarified by mentioning the programming language required.

The following methods and stylistic approaches will help the writer when preparing the duties and responsibilities section of job descriptions:

1. *Arrange duties and responsibilities sequentially.* This provides a logical flow or progression of activity. List the more predominant duties before those of lesser importance.

2. *State each duty or responsibility concisely and separately.* The descriptive phrases and statements should be self-contained and not overlap each other. For example, in the description of an accountant the statement "Makes all entries into the general ledger as well as payments of all invoices after which the accounts are consolidated" mixes several responsibilities. It can be better stated by three identifiable tasks:

   • "(What) makes all entries into the general ledger"

   • "(What) pays all invoices received during the prior week"

   • "(What) consolidates and balances the accounts on a weekly basis."

EXHIBIT 5

A Guide for the Preparation of Job Descriptions

Effective administration of salaries requires accurate job descriptions. A job description is a complete written record of the basic concepts of a given job, expressed in language that leaves no doubt as to the job's scope and limitations. This guide is intended primarily to give assistance in the preparation of initial drafts of job descriptions. The final drafts will be prepared in the Personnel Development Department.

A widely used practice today is to divide the job description into two sections: the basic responsibilities and the specific duties. It is frequently easier to draft the specific duties first and then summarize these to form the basic responsibilities.

Purpose (Job Summary)

The first item to be described in this section should be that of the line authority involved. This should then be followed by a two- or three-sentence summary of the *basic* responsibilities or purpose of the job. It is suggested that this section read as follows: "Under the direction (or supervision) of _____(the position exercising direct authority), is responsible for (two-or three-sentence summary)." An elaboration on these responsibilities is more properly contained in the Responsibilities section.

Responsibilities (Duties)

The duties of the position should be listed in the section in their approximate order of importance. A position might involve a series of operations that must be completed in a particular order and therefore might best be described in terms of the time sequence involved.

In preparing the details of the responsibilities, observe the following techniques:

1. Use brief and to-the-point statements.

2. Begin each sentence with an action verb.

3. Use the present tense.

4. Avoid verbs which do not specifically indicate the action involved. "Handles mail" is better expressed as "sorts mail" or "distributes mail."

5. Describe in brief and explicit sentences each major duty.

6. Describe those duties which might differentiate this job from other similar jobs.

7. Do not attempt to set down every detail of the job. Give only as much information as is necessary to define clearly what levels of skills, responsibility, and knowledge are required.

8. Include examples of any unusual duties, which occur only at certain intervals—monthly, quarterly, etc.—or as the occasion arises.

To be sure that the description accurately reflects the duties and responsibilities of the position, ask yourself these questions:

1. What is the general purpose of the job?

2. What are usual day-to-day duties performed (those of a recurring nature)?

3. What are other duties that occur at irregular intervals, but that are of a recurring nature?

4. Will examples of non-recurring duties clarify the description?

5. From whom (state title) is supervision received on a particular duty, if other than the person indicated in the Purpose (Job Summary) section?

6. What are the titles of individuals who normally would receive supervision from the person who holds this job?

7. To what extent will employees in this job plan their own activities?

8. What responsibility will this be for company funds that might be involved in any of the duties?

9. What office machines or equipment might be operated in the performance of these duties?

10. What records are maintained by persons in this job and what action is taken in record keeping?

11. What are the usual contacts made in this job?
    a. Within the company?
    b. Outside the company?

3. *Begin statements with action verbs.* Use "supervise," "design," "consolidate," "analyze." This is a matter of style. Statements that begin with qualifying phrases, double negatives, or forms of rhetoric, distract the reader from the main points. For example, do not write a statement describing one of the tasks of a quality control engineer, "In an effort to maintain a high level of acceptance of the product by the customer, conducts periodic product audits to determine variance from standards." Instead, the task is better stated, "Conducts weekly audits of the product by comparing its performance against quality standards established by the chief engineer."

4. *Use quantitative terms where possible.* "Daily," "weekly," "monthly" are preferable because they are more precise than "often," "occasional," "periodic."

5. *Avoid generalizations.* For example, to indicate that a supervisor "provides guidance and leadership to others" is vague. What kind of guidance and how is it provided? Which groups or individuals are currently getting the kind of guidance and leadership implied? This may be better stated to read, "Conducts weekly meetings with one's direct staff to review and discuss the department's activity and to develop future directions to follow."

6. *Use quantitative terms to indicate frequency or degree of duties performed.* For instance, if travel is required, indicate the amount of travel to give a measure of its significance. Write, "Travel on a weekly basis to inspect installations throughout the state." This is preferred to "Travel periodically throughout one's assigned area."

7. *Omit minor duties or occasional tasks common to all jobs.* Duties or tasks that are taken for granted can also be left out. For example, the secretarial task of "opening and arranging the daily mail for distribution to individual members of the office staff" can be omitted from the job description since it can be implied from the broader statement of "responsibility for incoming and outgoing mail."

Uniformity of style. Most persons, particularly supervisors and managers, have at some time written something to describe their jobs. This usually occurs in preparing résumés or in filling out those parts of applications for employment that ask for previous experience. Such writings have given these persons some experience in writing job descriptions. However, a well-written description is much more rigorous than a résumé. Moreover for the sake of clarity a series of descriptions that are formulated by the company or department should have uniform styles and formats.

The person who administers the job description program has a responsibility to preserve uniformity of style and format in descriptions even though a number of people may be involved in preparing them. In a small company, this person may be the personnel manager or a designated operating manager. In a large organization it may be a specialist, such as a job analyst. If an outside consultant has been retained to assist in the development of the job description program, preserving uniformity may be one of his or her responsibilities. A person in the company should be trained to acquire the necessary skills to maintain the program after the consultant has completed his or her work.

GUIDES FOR PREPARATION OF JOB DESCRIPTIONS

Exhibits 5 through 8 are designed as guides for those persons who are involved in the preparation of job descriptions. Photocopies of these exhibits can be made and distributed to the appropriate persons. These guides are in actual use at various companies, which have asked that they not be identified. They have been prepared by expert job analysts.

Exhibit 5, "Guide for the preparation of job descriptions," is intended for use by employees who are requested to write drafts of their own jobs.

Exhibit 6, "Guide to preparing management job descriptions," and Exhibit 7, "Guide for preparing non-management job descriptions" are directed to managers who are asked to write descriptions for employees under their responsibility.

Exhibit 8, "Glossary of terms used in job descriptions," should be distributed as reference material to all persons who write drafts of descriptions.

EXHIBIT 6

A Guide for Preparing
Management Job Descriptions

PREPARATION GUIDE—
MANAGEMENT DESCRIPTIONS

The management job description form from the Personnel Department should be completed in duplicate. One copy is for your records. The other should be forwarded to the administrator.

The form should be approved by the person currently in the position, if any, and must have the approval of at least two levels of supervision.

Content of Description

Section I

Basic Function
Summarize in three or four sentences the functions for which the position has been delegated responsibility and authority. State the overall objective of the position, what the position is to do, the reason for doing it and the scope of its intended result.

Section II

Personally Performed Responsibilities
Outline in this section those duties which are performed personally by the person holding the position. Duties which are supervised rather than personally performed are to be outlined under "Delegated Responsibilities."

A. **Planning and Policy Responsibility**

   Planning: To devise and project a course of action.

Policy: Broad objectives serving to direct the course of action toward the attainment of the company's goals. Policies should describe what the intended goal is.

B. **Procedural Responsibility**
Procedures: The manner or method of proceeding in the direction outlined by policy. It provides the detailed "how" by which policy is carried out.

C. **Other Personally Performed Responsibilities**
List all other important functions which the person currently holding the position performs. These statements should begin with an "action" verb which denotes the type of responsibility or authority exercised. Each duty can usually be made complete by answering WHAT? HOW? WHO? and WHEN? and occasionally WHERE? and WHY?

D. **Scope of Responsibilities**
Indicate the geographic area directly affected by the decisions required in this position, whether corporate, regional or local. One position may develop a policy which affects only a few employees, whereas another may develop a policy which affects all employees in the company. The same contrast may apply with respect to procedures.

Section III

Delegated Responsibilities
This section lists the jobs that the person in the position directly supervises, and the "Basic Functions" for each of these jobs. Included are direct subordinates only (excluding clerical), and not areas of the organization over which the position exercises staff or functional supervision.

Section IV

Supervision of Others
A. **Administrative**
This section should reveal the total number of employees reporting to the position for administrative as opposed to

functional work direction. In column (1) list the titles of all direct subordinates and in columns (2) and (3) indicate by classification the number of subordinate employees for whom each of the direct subordinates is responsible. Do not list an employee more than once.

B. **Functional (Staff)**
Some staff as well as line positions monitor or functionally supervise operations which report administratively to others. This may include monitoring policy and procedure performance by line personnel, providing advice and counsel to line personnel, etc. Describe briefly any assigned responsibilities which require the exercise of staff supervision including the type and approximate number of personnel who receive this supervision from the position being described.

Section V

Inside and Outside Relationships
Describe internal and external contacts which are required by the assigned responsibilities of the position.

Section VI

Traveling
Indicate if traveling is domestic or international and how many days of each.

Section VII

Remarks
Additional remarks to help clarify the job requirements are helpful. In describing any special qualifications such as formal training, kind of experience or particular abilities, give brief examples of why certain requirements are necessary. For example, if the job requires a degree in mathematics, briefly describe the need for such training.

EXHIBIT 7

A Guide for Preparing
Nonmanagement Job Descriptions

PREPARATION GUIDE— NONMANAGEMENT DESCRIPTIONS

The nonmanagement job description should be prepared in duplicate. One copy is for the supervisor's files and one copy is forwarded to corporate wage and salary or the field industrial relations office, whichever is appropriate.

Content of Description

Section I

Purpose of Job
Summarizes all of the duties listed under Section III. One or two sentences will usually explain the overall job function.

Example:
Determine on a continuing basis the manpower requirements to accomplish the expected workload by the use of published manpower standards. Plan, coordinate and regulate the development of personnel for the most effective and economical accomplishment of all phases of work within the service department.

Section II

Principal Functions of Job
List here, in order of importance, major functions of the job.

Section III

Duties of Job
List in the order shown in Section II, Principal Functions, more detail of each duty within a function. Tell not only *what* is done but also *how* and *why*. Give an estimate of the time needed to perform each duty.

Section IV

Requirements of Job
Complete those sections which are applicable. If not applicable, indicate "none."

Section V

Working Conditions
Unless there are unusual conditions such as noise, exposure to elements, or hazardous working situations, "none" should be indicated.

Approvals
The description should be signed by the employee whenever possible. Two levels of supervision immediately above the employee should approve the form.

EXHIBIT 8

Glossary of Terms Used in Job Descriptions

GLOSSARY OF TERMS USED IN JOB DESCRIPTIONS

ACT–To exert one's powers in such a way as to bring about an effect; to carry out a purpose.

ADMINISTER–To manage or direct the application or execution of; to administrate.

ADOPT–To take and apply or put into practice; to accept, as a report.

ADVISE–To give advice to; to recommend a course of action (not simply to tell or inform).

ANALYZE–To study the factors of a situation or problem in order to determine the solution or outcome. To study various unrelated facts to arrive at a conclusion.

ANTICIPATE–To foresee events, trends, consequences or problems.

APPRAISE–To evaluate as to quality, status, effectiveness.

APPROVE–To sanction officially, to accept as satisfactory; to ratify (thereby assuming responsibility for). Used only in the situation where individual has final authority.

ARRANGE–To place in proper order.

ASCERTAIN–To find out, or learn, for a certainty.

ASSEMBLE–To collect or gather together in a predetermined order; to fit together the parts of.

ASSIST–To lend aid; to help; to give support to.

ASSUME–To take to or upon oneself. To undertake.

ASSURE–To confirm; to make certain of; to state confidently.

ATTEND–To be present for the purpose of making a contribution.

AUDIT–Final and official examination of accounts.

AUTHORIZE–To empower; to permit; to establish by authority.

BALANCE–To arrange or prove so that the sum of one group equals the sum of another.

CALCULATE–To ascertain by computation.

CHECK–To examine; to compare for verification.

CIRCULATE–To disseminate; to distribute in accordance with a plan.

CLEAR–To obtain the concurrence, dissent or agreement of others prior to signature.

COLLABORATE–To work or act jointly with others.

COLLECT–To gather facts or data; to assemble; to accumulate.

COMPILE–To collect into a volume; to compose out of materials from other documents.

CONSOLIDATE–To combine into a single whole.

CONSULT–To seek the advice of another; to confer; to refer to.

CONTROL–To exercise directly guiding or restraining power over.

COOPERATE–To act or operate jointly with others (to collaborate).

COORDINATE–To bring into common action or condition.

CORRELATE–To establish a mutual or reciprocal relation.

DELEGATE–To entrust to the care or management of another.

DETERMINE–To fix conclusively or authoritatively; to decide; to make a decision.

DEVELOP–To evolve; to make apparent; to bring to light; to make more available or usable.

DIRECT–To regulate the activities or course of; to govern or control, to give guidance to.

DISCUSS–To exchange views for the purpose of arriving at a conclusion.

DISSEMINATE–To spread information or ideas.

DRAFT–To write or compose papers or documents usually in rough, preliminary form prior to final form. Often for clearance revision and approval by others.

EDIT–To revise and prepare as for publication.

EFFECTIVELY RECOMMENDS–Person recommending the action or procedure initiates the action or procedure, subject only to the routine or administrative control of some other person.

ESTABLISH–To set up; to institute; to place on a firm basis.

EVALUATE–To appraise; to ascertain the value of.

EXAMINE–To investigate; to scrutinize; to subject to inquiry by inspection or test.

EXECUTE–To give effect; to follow through to the end; complete.

EXERCISE–To bring to bear or employ actively, as exercise authority or influence.

EXPEDITE–To hasten the movement or progress of; to remove obstacles; to accelerate.

FACILITATE–To make easy or less difficult.

FOLLOW UP–To check the progress of; to see if results are satisfactory.

FORMULATE–To put into a systematized statement; to develop or devise a plan, policy or procedure.

FURNISH–To provide, supply or give.

IMPLEMENT–To carry out; to perform acts essential to the execution of a plan or program; to give effect to.

INFORM–To instruct; to communicate knowledge of.

INITIATE–To originate; to begin; to introduce for the first time, as a plan, policy or procedure.

INSPECT–To examine carefully and critically.

INSTRUCT–To impart knowledge to; to supply direction to.

INSTRUCTIONS–To furnish with directions, to inform.

DEFINITE INSTRUCTIONS–Precise in detail, explicit, limited in determining the course to follow.

GENERAL INSTRUCTIONS–Not precise, detailed, or specific.

INTENSIVE–Exhaustive or concentrated, extreme, high-degree.

INTERPRET–To explain the meaning of; to translate; to elucidate.

INTERVIEW–To question in order to obtain facts or opinions.

INVENTORY–To count and make a list of items.

INVESTIGATE–To inquire into systematically.

ISSUE–To distribute formally.

MAINTAIN–To hold or keep in any condition; to keep up-to-date or current, as records.

MAKE–To cause something to assume a designated condition.

MANAGE–To control and direct; to guide; to administer.

NOTIFY–To give notice to; to inform.

OBSERVE–To perceive or notice, watch.

OBTAIN–To gain possession of; to acquire.

OPERATE–To conduct or perform activity.

PARTICIPATE–To take part in.

PERFORM–To carry on to a finish; to accomplish; to execute.

PLAN–To devise or project a method or a course of action.

PREPARE–To make ready for a particular purpose.

PROCESS–To subject to some special treatment; to handle in accordance with prescribed procedures.

PROVIDE–To supply for use; to furnish; to take precautionary actions in view of a possible need.

PURCHASE–To buy or procure.

PURPOSE–To offer for consideration or adoption.

RECEIVE–To take something that is offered.

RECOMMEND–To advise a course of action.

RECOMMENDS – Suggests courses of action or procedures to other persons who have the primary responsibility for adopting and carrying out the actions or procedures recommended. Quotes what is recommended; the action or procedure is studied by the person receiving the recommendation, who then decides what course should be taken and initiates the resulting action or procedures.

RECORD–To register; to make a record of.

RELEASE–To permit the publication or dissemination of, at a specified date but not before.

RENDER–To furnish, contribute.

REPORT–To furnish information or data.

REPRESENT–To take the place of.

REQUIRE–To demand what must be accomplished

RESPONSIBILITY—Accountable for own decisions.

1. *Complete Responsibility* – Individual has complete authority to take whatever action he or she deems advisable or necessary, subject only to the policies or general rules laid down by his or her immediate supervisor.

2. *Delegated Responsibility* – Individual has the authority to take whatever action he or she deems advisable or necessary; he may initiate and carry out the action but is required to advise his superiors of the action taken when deemed necessary. Must inform superiors of nonroutine situations.

3. *General Responsibility* – The individual is required to gain approval of his or her supervisor before proceeding with the action which he or she deems necessary or advisable.

REVIEW–To go over or examine critically. Usually with a view to approval or dissent. Analyze results for the purpose of giving an opinion.

REVISE–To make a new, improved or up-to-date version of.

ROUTINE–Regular procedure, course, or normal course of business or official duties.

NONROUTINE–Irregular or infrequent situations that arise relating to business or official duties. Characteristic of higher-level jobs.

SCAN–To examine point by point. To scrutinize.

SCHEDULE–To plan a timetable; to set specific times for.

SCREEN–To examine closely, generally so as to separate one group or class from another.

SECURE–To get possession of; to obtain.

SEE–To make certain of; to learn through observation.

SELECT–Chosen from a number of others of similar kind.

SIGN–To affix a signature to.

STIMULATE–To excite, rouse or spur on.

STUDY–To consider attentively; to ponder or fix the mind closely upon a subject.

SUBMIT–To present for decision, information for judgment of others.

SUPERVISE–To oversee for directions. To inspect with authority. To guide and instruct with immediate responsibility for purpose of performance; to superintend; to lead.

1. *Direct Supervision* – Involves guidance and direction over individuals who report to and are directly responsible to the supervisor. Includes supervision of work, training, and personnel functions.

2. *Close Supervision* – Individual does not use own initiative. Is instructed by supervisor as to the solution and selection of the proper procedures to follow.

3. *Limited Supervision* – Individual proceeds on his own initiative in compliance with policies, practices, and procedures prescribed by his or her immediate supervisor.

4. *General Supervision* – Involves guidance and direction actually carried out by the intermediate supervisor.

5. *Supervision of Work* – Includes: work distribution, scheduling, training, answering questions related to work, assistance in solving problems, etc. Does not include any personnel functions such as: salaries, discipline, promotions, etc.

6. *Training Responsibility* – Involves advice, information and guidance on specialized matters; involves no authority. Gives instruction in regard to procedures.

SURVEY–To determine the form, extent, or position of a situation, usually in connection with gathering of information.

TRAIN–To increase skill or knowledge by capable instruction. Usually in relation to a predetermined standard.

VERIFY–To prove to be true or accurate; to confirm or substantiate; to test or check the accuracy of.

THE ROLES OF
THE PARTICIPANTS IN
DESCRIPTION WRITING

The writing of job descriptions requires the participation of a number of persons and groups in the company. To serve fully its intended purpose, a job description program should meet the needs of the following groups:

The top management of the company
The supervisory groups
The employees
The job analyst.

In smaller companies the job analyst may be a person who has other responsibilities, such as a personnel manager, office manager, or highest-ranking operations manager.

THE ROLE OF GENERAL MANAGEMENT

General management identifies the need and the purpose for a job description program. Without such focus, a program will not materialize, or proceed with any sense of purpose.

Top management must establish the general policies and issue directives. It must communicate such information to these areas of the company where necessary. For instance, if descriptions are restricted to one purpose, such as recruiting new employees, management's communication may be limited to those departments which are engaged in recruiting.

Usually, however, descriptions serve broader purposes such as the development and maintenance of a wage and salary administration program, smoothing the work flow, manpower planning and the like. In this case, all operating managers and supervisors must be informed.

Communication of general management's policy need not include detailed information concerning administrative procedures, formats, or methods. It should include the essential elements, such as:

The purpose of the program

The delegated responsibility to the person or group who will implement and administer such program

The time within which preparation of the descriptions is expected to be completed

The responsibility and authority for resolving problems and the authority for final approval.

THE ROLE OF SUPERVISORS

In a comprehensive program several levels of supervisory management will become involved. The immediate supervisor establishes the specific duties and responsibilities of the job that is being described. He or she assists the job analyst in defining the primary tasks of the work. The supervisor's work unit is first outlined. Then, the individual jobs are identified. Following that, the job responsibilities are outlined. Finally, all the persons in that unit are classified into the jobs that have been outlined.

The supervisor has the responsibility for communicating the need, methods, purpose, procedures and the process of description writing to the employees. This is particularly important when the program requires employee participation.

The supervisor must agree with the job analyst (or person who writes the final descriptions) that the final descriptions do show the identity and content of each job. A description cannot be considered complete and approved until the supervisor concurs that it represents what is expected from the person assigned to that job.

Cooperation between the supervisor and the analyst must be obtained. They should work on the writing of job descriptions as partners. The supervisor should make it easy for the job analyst to see the work environment to encourage close examination of all jobs.

THE EXTENT OF PARTICIPATION BY EMPLOYEES IN A JOB DESCRIPTION PROGRAM

In large organizations top management often wants the participation of employees in the process of job description writing. In relatively small companies the opposite is often true. This is not necessarily because management doesn't want to encourage participation. It is due to the absence of distinct organizational units, functional specialization, and definable units of work that do not change their characteristics.

Wide Participation by Employees

The primary role of an individual employee is to cooperate with the direct supervisor in outlining the details of his or her job. Each individual prepares an initial draft of the job description to include the essential duties, tasks and responsibilities of the job. Since employees usually don't have expertise in writing even rough drafts of job descriptions, the program administrator or the job analyst provides specific guides to make this task easier for the employee and also to make the drafts uniform. Typical guides for this purpose include questionnaires, interview forms and logs. These are discussed and illustrated later in this section.

Occasionally employees are included in the review process of all drafts. Management may consider this desirable. Where a union agreement is involved, a review procedure that includes representatives of the employees is normally mandatory.

This approach has two advantages. First, employee review ensures that the described duties, responsibilities and interactions truly reflect the work and its environment. This attitude is based on the belief that a person who does the job knows more about it than other persons who are not directly involved.

The second advantage is centered on the belief that participative management leads to a more effective work force. Such participation does not necessarily produce better descriptions, but they have greater credibility which leads to better acceptance and use.

THE ROLE OF THE JOB ANALYST

Responsibilities include:

- Delineation of the organization, its divisions, departments, sections, and lesser units of work.

- Determination of the need for generic or for specific job descriptions to suit the purpose for which they are intended.

- Development of the guides to collect information for each unit of work, from which draft descriptions may be prepared.

- Development of administrative procedures, communication materials, and training vehicles to inform supervisors and employees of their roles and participation.

- Coordination of all interdivisional and interdepartmental efforts to achieve the desired format, schedules, and commitments.

- Centralization of information about overlapping and interactions among sections and departments.

- Identification of conflicting information in order to present recommendations for final resolution by senior management.

- Maintenance of central information files where all approved descriptions are kept and cataloged for reference.

- Establishment of periodic audits to ensure that descriptions are kept current.

5

JOB
ANALYSIS

Through job analysis the description writer secures information about a particular job so that the writer can describe it accurately and establish realistic specifications and requirements for it. The information with which the writer is concerned relates to the job and not to its present holder; the analyst gathers information in four areas:

1. The identity of the job in the organizational structure. This includes its title, reporting responsibility and accountability, its location, whether geographic or organizational.

2. The essential tasks, duties and responsibilities of the job and the work that is being performed: *what* is being performed, *how* it is performed and for what purpose it is performed.

3. The degree of skills, knowledge and individual abilities that are required from a jobholder to provide an acceptable level of performance.

4. The working conditions, particularly if these conditions are not normal for the general class of job.

TECHNIQUES IN JOB ANALYSIS

There are four methods that the analyst can use to collect information:

1. Interviews. The analyst discusses with one or more job incumbents all the details of the work. The analyst uses a checklist (described later) to guide the discussion. He or she takes notes of responses and subsequently compiles them into the format of a job description.

The analyst does not need to interview all holders of a particular job. A representative sample is enough. For instance, if a certain kind of job is staffed with ten individuals, it should be sufficient to interview two or three of them. The supervisor can help identify the two or three persons who represent the most and the least proficient or experienced members of the group. The analyst can then establish minimum and maximum job specifications.

The interview technique has certain advantages:

- It establishes direct and open participation of employees.

- It gives the analyst a better understanding of the job.

- It allows for examination and clarification of ambiguous or complex areas of work that cannot be easily communicated.

There are some disadvantages in job analysis interviews:

- Some employees may feel threatened and not comfortable enough to provide adequate information.

- The interviews may dwell on the most current elements of the work and neglect the broader aspects of the job.

- There is a tendency for the employee and the supervisor to concentrate on the requirements that describe the person holding the job instead of the job itself. Furthermore, the supervisor may stress what he or she wishes an employee would do instead of what the employee actually does.

2. Job observation. In this ʼtechnique the analyst merely observes several job incumbents as they perform their duties. Occasionally the analyst may inquire about a certain element of work. During such observation, careful notes should be taken from which one later writes a job description.

Among the advantages of this technique are the following:

- Through observation the analyst gains firsthand familiarity with the work.

- The analyst can observe important working conditions that are sometimes distinguishing features of certain jobs.

- The analyst can observe several jobs at one time without interfering with the flow of work.

There are certain disadvantages:

- Some employees may be ill at ease when being watched.

- Intangible dimensions of work, such as its creative elements, mental requirements or human interactions, are not readily observable.

• Adequate observation of a job where routine activities are the exception can be very time-consuming. For example, to observe fully the work of a supervisor the analyst would need to accompany that individual for days or perhaps weeks to become familiar with all the elements of the job.

3. Job questionnaires. The method used most often for job analysis is the comprehensive questionnaire. It is distributed to all employees in a department. They complete and return it to the supervisor or analyst. Not all companies which use this technique have the job questionnaires filled out by employees. They may be completed by supervisors or managers. This is the practice where management has decided not to involve employees in the preparation of their own job descriptions..

Among the advantages of this method are the following:

• Questionnaires are an efficient and time-saving method to collect large amounts of information. Of course, the questionnaire must be properly designed and introduced.

• Questionnaires are effective tools where the jobs to be analyzed are well structured.

• Where jobs are located in geographically scattered areas, the analyst can collect information without travel.

• Written responses to questionnaires provide a permanent record of all reported facts. These are expressed by the participants rather than by the informal notes of the analyst.

Some of the disadvantages of questionnaires are:

• They eliminate contact and discussion between the analyst and the employee. Written answers may miss essential points.

• Great care is required to design effective questionnaires.

• Questionnaires take time to complete.

• Problems of interpretation can arise for the person who completes the questionnaires as well as for the analyst who has to correlate the responses.

4. Employee log. The fourth method has each employee keep a log of tasks and activities over a specified period of time. This method is acceptable where the work is routine and repeats itself in a short period of time, a week or, in some cases, a month. Production, clerical, office administration, or service and maintenance jobs lend themselves to keeping logs.

The log method does not provide the analyst with adequate information when the work is highly varied, or where the tasks do not repeat themselves in short periods of time. This is clearly the case in supervisory and managerial positions, sales and marketing jobs, and in professional or creative types of work.

The advantages of this method:

• Time is saved by the analyst in collecting large amounts of information about a large number of jobs.

• Employees can write in a log the variety of their routine tasks without having to interpret ambiguous questions.

• The method bypasses the reluctance of some employees to participate in job interviews.

There are some disadvantages:

• No personal contact between the analyst and the employee.

• The analyst cannot observe factors that affect the performance of a job.

• Employees may suspect that the purpose of the log is time studies from which management will set production standards.

• The method is limited to routine and repetitive jobs.

SELECTING THE BEST JOB ANALYSIS METHOD

To determine the best analysis technique, these factors should be considered:

• *Types of jobs*: Supervisory and professional jobs lend themselves to questionnaires and interviews. Routine work can be addressed through observation and logs.

• *Access of analyst to the work place*: Remote sales and service work can best be addressed through questionnaires and logs. Interviews and observation may be more convenient for home office jobs.

• *Prior preparation by the analyst*: Questionnaire preparation requires considerable design time and trial. Logs are usually less time-consuming because they need not be as elaborate. Interviews and observation are less cumbersome provided sufficient thought is given to what information need be collected.

EXHIBIT 9

Worksheet for Job Analysis

1. **Job identification**

    a. Name of organizational unit_____

    b. Current title of job_____

    c. Location_____

    d. Reporting relationship_____

2. **Sources of manpower**

    a. Sources of current jobholders_____

    _____

    _____

    b. Prior experience_____

    _____

    c. Previous jobs_____

    _____

    d. Education_____

    e. Years in jobs_____

    f. In prior jobs_____

3. **Work performed**

    a. Specific, frequently performed tasks_____

    _____

    _____

b. Responsibilities _____

_____

c. Supervisory scope _____

d. Interaction _____

e. Who gives direction _____

f. Which tasks are supervised _____

_____

g. Which are not _____

_____

h. How is quality checked _____

i. How reviewed _____

4. **Physical conditions**

a. Conditions surrounding the work area _____

_____

b. What are hours worked _____

c. Rest periods _____

d. Environmental conditions _____

5. **Skills required**

a. Mental _____

b. Manual _____

c. Interpersonal _____

6. **Knowledge required**

How are skills acquired (school, special courses, experience, training) _____

_____

_____

7. **Special requirements**

   a. Travel _____

   b. Isolation _____

   c. Night work _____

   d. Long hours _____

   e. Implicit conditions _____

8. **Accountability**

   a. For equipment _____

   b. Assets _____

   c. Profit margins _____

   d. Cash _____

   e. Expenditure _____

   f. Information _____

   g. Outside relations _____

9. **Organizational framework**

   How does the job fit into the organization: vertically, hori-

   zontally? _____

_____

_____

_____

- *Employee acceptance*: The interview method is least threatening since it allows the analyst to explain, and to respond to each individual. Questionnaires, logs and observation may be counterproductive if not preceded by effective communication to the employees.

Most experienced analysts believe that the job questionnaire method is the most effective. The questionnaire can be fortified by follow-up interviews on a selective basis. In this way, the job analyst can overcome the limitations of one by combining it with another.

Exhibit 9 outlines nine distinct areas of information for job analysis. From these the analyst can prepare sound and comprehensive job descriptions.

6

DESIGNING FORMS
FOR JOB ANALYSIS

An important step in job analysis is to identify clearly the reporting relationships within the company. The job analyst should first outline the organizational framework in which all jobs are located. One way to make the relationships and locations of all jobs clear is by drawing organization charts. Though most employees know to whom they report and who reports to them, conditions arise which make it more difficult for the job analyst to define reporting relationships or locate jobs on a chart in a way that is acceptable to management. This occurs because certain employees have composite responsibilities. Some of their tasks are supervised by one manager and some by another. This frequently occurs in smaller companies. It need not interfere with good job analysis provided that the two managers agree on the distribution of responsibilities and the allocation of time of that employee between the functions.

Another condition that makes job analysis more difficult occurs when an employee performs two distinctly different jobs, both reporting to the same manager. At certain times the employee performs one job and at other times another. The analyst should recognize that these are two separate jobs, each of which should be separately described. The fact that one person has both jobs should be considered as temporary. Eventually, there will be two separate jobs, each of which will be staffed by one employee.

The analyst examines and portrays the existing structure and jobs as they are. As the organization changes, however, so should the descriptions. Organizational structures are shown either by a chart or by an outline. Exhibit 10 shows an organizational diagram, or chart, of a manufacturing plant that has four product lines. It graphically shows the positions and reporting relationships of the product managers to the plant manager and the relationships of the employee relations, purchasing, operations planning, and service managers to the plant manager and to the product manager.

Exhibit 11 shows a diagram of the departmental structure of one of the managers, the employee relations manager, whose relationship to the plant manager and product line managers is depicted on the organizational diagram in Exhibit 10. These diagrams are constructed by the job analyst to help in the actual analysis, the details of which will eventually be incorporated in the final job descriptions.

ORGANIZATIONAL OUTLINES

Large organizations find it helpful to use organizational outlines that use codes for the various jobs. This makes it easier to cross-reference jobs, to code them, and to maintain files of jobs. Such coded organizational outlines are partic-

EXHIBIT 10

Organizational Diagram—Manufacturing Plant

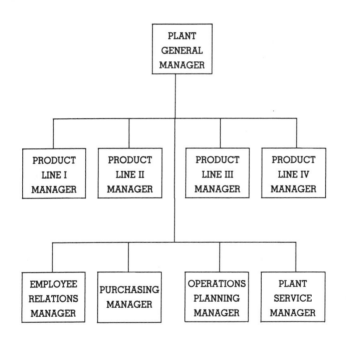

EXHIBIT 11

Departmental Diagram—Employee Relations Department

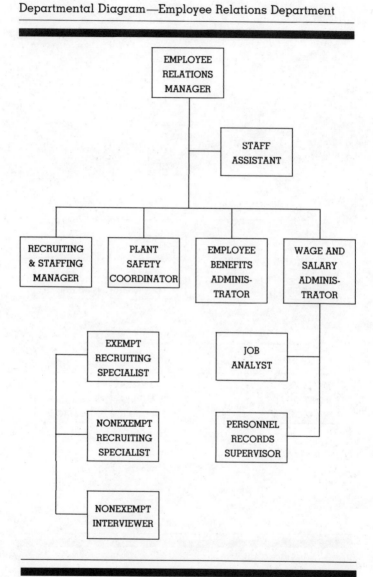

ularly useful in elaborate filing systems that use electronic data processing systems.

Exhibit 12 shows a typical organizational outline. Each job or position that was graphically depicted in Exhibits 10 and 11 is shown on this coded outline form. The plant manager, for instance, is given a 1 code. The product line managers, who report to the plant manager, each retain the code 1 and have the numbers 1 through 4 to show their identities as well as relationships.

The jobs under the departmental managers (shown in Exhibits 16 and 17) each indicate their identities and relationships through the company by codes.

PREPARATION OF INTERVIEW FORMS

Exhibit 9 provides a work sheet for an analyst to gather information for a job analysis. The items on this work sheet are the same ones that the analyst can use to design forms for the interview and questionnaire methods of getting information, from which job descriptions can be developed.

While the interviewer may not ask all of the questions shown in Exhibit 9 either in interviews or on questionnaires, most of them should be put into an interview form. Exhibit 13, "Interview form for collection of job description data" shows the form that one company uses to gather data through interviews for clerical, supervisory and administrative positions.

Exhibit 14 is a similar interview form used by another company. Both gather essentially the same data. The interview form in Exhibit 13 is more tightly structured than that in Exhibit 14. The latter gives the analyst more latitude in posing questions and interacting with the person being interviewed.

EXHIBIT 12

Coded Organizational Outlines

---

1. Plant General Manager

    1.1 Product Line I Manager
    1.2 Product Line II Manager
    1.3 Product Line III Manager
    1.4 Product Line IV Manager

    1.5 Employee Relations Manager
        1.5.1 Staff Assistant
        1.5.2 Recruiting & Staffing Manager
            1.5.1.1 Exempt Recruiting Specialist
            1.5.1.2 Nonexempt Recruiting Specialist
            1.5.1.3 Nonexempt Interviewer
        1.5.3 Plant Safety Coordinator
        1.5.4 Employee Benefits Administrator
        1.5.5 Wage & Salary Administrator
            1.5.5.1 Job Analyst
            1.5.5.2 Personnel Records Supervisor

    1.6 Operations Planning Manager Etc.

Before beginning the interviews the analyst should study the organizational chart and existing job titles. He or she should inform the supervisors of the nature of the interview and the time that will be required. In turn, the supervisors should tell each employee to be interviewed of its purpose and the time that it will take place.

EXHIBIT 13

Interview Form for Collection of Job Description Data
for Clerical, Supervisory and Administrative Positions

TYPE OF JOB

Clerical ___Administrative ___Supervisory ___Foreman ___

A. 1. Interviewer_____ 2. Date_____

    3. Person interviewed_____

B. 1. Present job title_____

    2. Suggested job title_____

    3. Immediate superior_____

    4. Job title of immediate superior_____

    5. Department_____ 6. Job location_____

    7. Number of employees on this job_____

C. 1. Describe most important duties that the employee or
employees on this job perform daily. If important duties are performed at less frequent intervals, describe
and give the frequency of performance.

    2. Describe the secondary duties that an employee on
this job performs at periodic intervals, such as weekly,
monthly, quarterly, etc., and state frequency of performance. Describe duties employee may perform.

D. 1. Equipment for office machine operations

    2. Factory or shop machines and equipment (foremen)

E. 1. Describe the working conditions.

F. 1. Describe the formal education or its equivalent required for satisfactory performance of this job.

   2. Specify the prior special training or education necessary before an employee is assigned to this job or training necessary immediately after assignment.

   3. Describe any job experience required and indicate the number of weeks, months, or years needed to obtain such experience and state whether in this organization or elsewhere.

G. 1. Describe the proximity, extent and closeness of supervision received by an employee on this job. To what degree does the immediate supervisor outline methods to be followed, results to be accomplished, check work progress, handle exceptional cases, check job performance?

   2. Describe the kind of supervision the employee or employees on this job give the other employees. What is the degree of accountability for results in terms of methods, work accomplished, and personnel?

   3. How many employees are supervised directly? _____ Indirectly? _____

H. 1. Responsibility for accuracy and seriousness of error. What is the seriousness of error on this job? Who would discover it? Do errors affect the work of employee making mistake, others in the same department, other departments, persons outside the organization?

I. 1. Responsibility for confidential data. State the type of confidential data handled, whether personnel, salaries, policy, business secrets, etc.

J. 1. Responsibility for money or things of monetary value. State the type of responsibility and the approximate amount of money employee must safeguard.

K. 1. Describe the kind of personal contacts made by employees as he/she performs job. Is contact with persons in the department, in other departments, outside the organization? Importance of contacts to organization should be described.

L. 1. Describe the complexity of the job. What is the degree of independent action permitted the employee? What decisions is employee permitted to make?

M. 1. Describe the type and amount of dexterity or motor skill required in the performance of the job. Indicate job duties where dexterity is required.

N. 1. Describe the degree of repetitive detail required of the employee. Determine the possibility for the experience of boredom on the job.

O. 1. List any unusual physical requirements of this job. Vision, strength, appearance, pressure.

P. 1. Obtain any forms or written procedures which will make it easy to write a job description. If standard practices for job exist, obtain these and check against actual job duties performed.

EXHIBIT 14

Interview Sheet for Collection of Data for Job Descriptions

INTERVIEW SHEET

Conducted by: _____
Date: _____

Title:_____   Immediate Supervisor:_____

_____   _____

_____   _____

Unit:_____   Time in Job:_____

_____   _____

_____   _____

Department:_____   Previous Job:_____

_____   _____

_____   _____

Division:_____   _____

_____   _____

_____   _____

Incumbent_____   _____

_____   _____

_____   _____

Duties Usually Performed:	**Approximate % of Time**

Occasionally Performed	Frequency
Most Complex or Difficult Duty Performed:	
General Purpose:	

Minimum specifications (for entry into job)

1. **Education Required:**

2. **Experience Required:**
    A. **Related**–(on jobs of lesser degree within our company)
        Position   **Time**

    B. **Related**–outside our company (indicate nature of work)

    C. **General Business Experience** (unrelated–indicate time period)

3. **Skills Required** (equipment or special courses):

4. **Other Requirements:**

Equipment or Skills Learned on Job:

_____

_____

_____

Development Time:

1. Time to reach satisfactory performance (breaking-in time)

2. Time to reach normal supervision:

Extent to Which Instructions Cover Work:

Judgment or Accuracy Required	Frequency	Effect of Error	Probability of Error

Who Checks Work	Extent and/or How Work Is Checked	Frequency

Contacts Required to Perform Job Duties (include frequency, purpose and method of contact):

1. With persons in the company:

2. With persons outside the company:

Working Conditions (Include description of environment and physical activity and percentages of time spent lifting, typing, etc.):

Other Comments:

While on-site discussions let the interviewer observe working conditions and allow for demonstrations, they can be distracting and embarrassing to the employee. It is preferable for the analyst to have private interviews in a neutral environment. These can be followed by visits to the work site where demonstrations can be made and conditions discussed.

INTERVIEWING PRACTICES

To relieve tension, the interviewer should begin with some casual remarks, and then should explain the purpose of the interview and how it will be conducted. Also, the jobholder should be told how the information collected will be used.

The analyst should prepare the questions carefully to avoid hidden meanings or ambiguities. Encourage the employee to speak and give him or her sufficient time to answer or to demonstrate a particular point.

The tone of the interview should be conversational provided it remains focused on the subject. The interviewer need take only occasional notes. This is less distracting and does not threaten the conversation as would be true if all thoughts were written down.

At the end of the interview, the employee should be given the opportunity to offer further information or to raise any questions. Immediately after the interview, the analyst should write out complete notes, observations and information. The interview form and work sheet are valuable tools for this purpose as they provide uniform formats with which information from different interviews can be compared. Actual writing of a job description will not begin until several interviews have been completed.

HOW TO COLLECT
DATA THROUGH THE
JOB QUESTIONNAIRE

A questionnaire must be preceded by clear instructions on how it should be filled out. The analyst should include with the job questionnaire an explanation of it, its purposes, what will be done with the data and the procedures to be followed. It is a responsibility of the operating manager also to explain to employees the purposes of the job questionnaire and to clarify any issues that might arise.

Exhibit 15 shows an actual questionnaire used to collect data that the job analyst can use in the preparation of job descriptions.

This questionnaire is filled out by the holder of the job for which the analyst is preparing a description. On the first page of the "Position Description Questionnaire" shown in Exhibit 15 is a section that explains to the employee the purpose of the questionnaire.

Another section instructs him or her in the procedures to be followed, including the advice that questions about the questionnaire form should be directed to the employee's supervisor.

Also, this questionnaire has a section to be completed by the employee's supervisor. This company requires the supervisor to approve the questionnaire that has been filled out by the employee.

Should there be any differences of opinion between the employee and the supervisor about the job, these differences should be resolved between them before the form is sent to the job analyst. Both employee and supervisor are required to sign the form.

EXHIBIT 15

Questionnaire Form for Collection of Data
for Preparation of Job Descriptions

**POSITION
DESCRIPTION
Questionnaire**

Classification
Title_____

Code_____Date Received_____

Clerical_____Technical_____

Comments_____

_____

_____

(WAGES & SALARY CONTROL USE ONLY)

Employee Name_____Clock No._____Date_____

Position Title_____Mail Station_____

Department_____Supervisor_____

Explanation

Job Analysis is the process of determining and reporting pertinent information relating to the nature of a specific job. It is the determination of tasks which comprise the job, together with skills, knowledge, responsibilities, etc., required for successful performance and which differentiate the job from all others.

Procedure

Employee: Complete entries above and Section I on pages 2 and 3. Describe in *detail* the *primary* or *most important duties* that you as an employee perform. List the job duties in clear, concise sentences. Indicate the frequency (day, week, month) and amount of time spent performing these primary job duties. Be certain that you provide sufficient information about each specific duty to enable persons unfamiliar with your work to understand what the duty entails. Questions should be directed to your supervisor.

Supervisor: Complete Section II on page 4.

Section I

1. Duty (what)_____

   Procedure (how)_____

   _____

   _____

   Reason for duty (why)_____

   _____

   Frequency _____and Percentage _____estimate of time spent performing duty.

2. Duty (what)_____

   Procedure (how)_____

   _____

   _____

   Reason for duty (why) _____

   _____

   Frequency _____and Percentage _____estimate of time spent performing duty.

3. Duty (what)_____

   Procedure (how)_____

   _____

   _____

   Reason for duty (why)_____

   _____

   Frequency _____and Percentage _____estimate of time spent performing duty.

4. Duty (what)_____

   Procedure (how)_____

   _____

   _____

   Reason for duty (why)_____

   _____

   Frequency _____and Percentage _____estimate of
   time spent performing duty.

5. Duty (what)_____

   Procedure (how)_____

   _____

   _____

   Reason for duty (why)_____

   _____

   Frequency _____and Percentage _____estimate of
   time spent performing duty.

6. Duty (what)_____

   Procedure (how)_____

   _____

   _____

   Reason for duty (why)_____

   _____

   Frequency _____and Percentage _____estimate of
   time spent performing duty.

What machines/equipment are you required to use proficiently
on your job? How much time per day or week is spent using
each machine or piece of equipment listed?

Machine/Equipment   **Time in Use**

_____   _____

_____   _____

_____   _____

What are the most difficult decisions to make? What do you consider the most important task(s) you perform?

_____

_____

_____

_____

_____

Describe the working conditions which may cause a feeling of pressure or discomfort. Consider environment, distractions and interference which might make completion of task(s) difficult:

_____

_____

_____

_____

_____

Describe the personal contacts you are required to make to perform the job.

Who? (Title?)_____   Reason_____

_____

Who? (Title?)_____   Reason_____

_____

Who? (Title?)_____   Reason_____

_____

Signature_____
Employee

Section II

Section I reviewed and approved by_____
(Immediate Supervisor)

Comments:_____

_____

_____

_____

_____

_____

_____

_____

_____

Errors which may occur in this job are: (Check one)

_____Easily detected in normal routine of checking results.

_____Detected in subsequent steps such as balancing, exception reports, etc.

Give example:_____

_____Not detected until they have caused other departments considerable inconvenience.

Give example:_____

_____Not detected until they have caused considerable inconvenience to another company.

Give example:_____

Describe responsibility of the occupant of this position for work of other employees. (Check one)

_____No responsibility for work of others. May show other employees how to perform a task or assist in indoctrination of new employees.

_____Guides and instructs other employees, assigning, checking, and maintaining the flow of work.

LIMITATIONS
OF JOB INFORMATION

Job information is primarily concerned with the job and not with the incumbent, the person currently holding the job. Nevertheless, analysts can confuse incumbent attributes and characteristics with job specifications. This is understandable when certain specifications cannot be quantified. The cause of the confusion might be reflected in one or more of the following:

Behavioral requirements of the job

Interactive and interpersonal relations

Personality attributes such as creativity, concern for detail, etc.

Care should be taken to distinguish whether these intangible qualities are:

inherent to the requirements of the job, in which case they are job-related, or

contribute to the successful performance of an incumbent in that job, in which case they are incumbent-related.

To illustrate: Consider the job specifications for an operating-room nurse. Compassion is a desirable characteristic of the occupation of nursing. It is an intangible quality that is difficult to measure or describe in a formal description or specification.

It is questionable, however, whether the quality of compassion contributes to a higher level of medical care in an *operating* room. It appears, therefore, that compassion is not a job-related attribute. Instead, it can contribute to a higher degree of patient acceptance and comfort and, thus, is incumbent-related. The job analyst needs to exercise discretion and objectivity in determining where these differences lie.

THE USES OF JOB DESCRIPTIONS

Once formal job descriptions gain acceptance, managers find other practical applications for them in addition to the most common use in wage and salary administration programs. A brief discussion of the uses of job descriptions in such programs as well as other uses will shed some further light on results that can be obtained through written job descriptions.

Job descriptions provide the primary tool with which units of work can be identified and defined. These units provide a way to compare one job to another and to rank them. Job descriptions help the process of job evaluation.

Jobs are rank ordered by using criteria that management considers significant to the success of the organization. Typical criteria are the skills and efforts required to perform a particular job and its responsibility.

Job evaluation provides management with a tool with which to establish a rate of pay for each job relative to all others. The rate of pay can be a fixed amount or a range from a minimum to a maximum. Therefore, job evaluation and resultant wage and salary scales must be based on clear definitions of work and responsibility. Careful job analysis also assures consistency in setting pay rates among individual workers and groups of employees. When significant changes in responsibility or in the organization take place, the job descriptions should be revised. These, then, can be reevaluated and assigned new pay levels or salary ranges.

USES IN RECRUITMENT SELECTION AND STAFFING

Properly drawn job descriptions can help in the search for qualified workers, employees, supervisors and managers. For instance, writing an advertisement for a specific job is simplified by summarizing the job description and its specifications.

When selecting individuals for jobs, interviewers will find that job descriptions will help the entire interview process by focusing it on relevant facts. The interviewer can seek out the prior experiences of a job candidate and try to match them to the tasks and responsibilities in a job description.

The generic types of descriptions are generally more helpful in recruiting than are specific descriptions. The recruiter seeks individuals with experiences and qualifications that are adaptable or transferable to the broad statements of work and responsibility in generic descriptions.

USES IN MANPOWER PLANNING, TRAINING AND DEVELOPMENT

When a company expands, new manpower becomes a necessity. In a long-range plan, the precise form of the future organization may not be readily known. However, the technical, managerial and specialized skills can be given in the broad terms that usually appear in generic description.

A manager who wants to adapt an existing work force for the future needs of the company can prepare generic job descriptions that would satisfy these needs. A comparison of current and future descriptions can provide a manager with a fair estimate of where to find personnel with the necessary qualifications. Furthermore, the manager can discover specific training and development needs and can then plan training programs for the current labor force that will prepare it for the future.

Manpower training and development is also relevant to today's operations. For instance, a manager can compare the qualifications of incumbents with those outlined in a specific job description and identify the needs for individual or group training efforts.

USES IN PERFORMANCE APPRAISAL

The latest approaches in performance appraisal stress the importance of motivation and setting of goals or objectives for each employee. As a result, job descriptions as tools for performance appraisal are no longer as important as they once were. Nevertheless, the job description remains the main reference on which to base performance standards.

The degree to which employees perform their duties is the basis upon which they are appraised. The job description provides the manager with a tool to determine whether the employee is performing all the specified duties and responsibilities.

As was pointed out earlier, certain behavioral aptitudes cannot be readily included in a description: degrees of creativity, resourcefulness, analytical expertise, alertness, and the like. These aptitudes may be important criteria for assessing performance. Therefore, the manager should not use job descriptions as the only basis to measure performance.

Work-Flow Analysis and Organizational Design

Job descriptions can be used in work-flow analysis. Work-flow analysts do not indicate "who does what." Instead they outline "what should be done," the steps and procedures between input and output. The work-flow analyst can use job descriptions as the starting point to construct a flow diagram. Once the analyst has completed the diagram that includes the operations and steps in the work, these diagrams can help the job analyst discover tasks that may not have been evident in job descriptions. This new information can be used to further refine the descriptions. A strong interdependence should develop between the work flow and the job analysts.

This interdependence alerts managers to the need for redesigning jobs to get work done in a more effective way. This may result in the tasks, duties and responsibilities being rearranged from one description to another.

IN SEARCH OF
THE TOP-NOTCH EMPLOYEE

Now that you know just what kind of job description program and interviewing process you're going to use, you have to go out and find a candidate pool to dip into. Here's a look at the most common methods of conducting your search, from advertising to networking.

THE MASS MEDIA

To a large extent, the type of job opening will determine how much money will be spent on the advertising campaign to find the right person. But the point is: No matter what the position may be in the company, you will want to find the best man or woman for the job. More times than not, companies turn to the classified advertising pages of the major newspapers in the cities in which the company resides. In New York City, for example, the *New York Times* devotes an entire section of its Sunday edition just to classified advertisements. In addition, the *Times* has two other sections—one strictly for educational and medical openings, and the other for professionals—full of display advertisements of job offerings.

When writing the copy for an advertisement, it's important for you to coordinate with the company personnel director to make certain that the advertisement reflects the job opening accurately, complete with job description and salary range. Writing these classified advertisements properly can make the difference between getting good applicants and getting excellent applicants.

Other Advertising Methods

Beyond newspapers, which are probably the most common media for job advertising, there are other segments of the mass media. Trade publications and professional journals within your firm's field or industry are always excellent places to advertise. By advertising in a particular magazine, you've already narrowed your field of applicants just to people within a specific industry. They are probably familiar with your company and your products, and already know of your standing in the field. That can save time and expense when going through applicants' résumés.

More recently, companies are turning to electronic communications. Radio and television advertising has become more popular in spreading the word about job openings. You can view this approach as not only telling the general public that your particular company is doing well—hiring new people to fill jobs—but that you can reach an audience that is usually much larger than a newspaper's readership. Usually, radio and television advertising is limited to only entry-level or blue-collar type jobs. It's extremely rare when managers are recruited in such a fashion.

AGENCIES

Employment agencies have become more in vogue in recent years due to the increase in job-hopping. One caution with such agencies: Be careful. Many of these firms do nothing more than scan the classified sections of newspapers and then try to place job applicants in those positions. Then they charge your firm a fee for services rendered. That fee depends on the job opening, but it's usually a percentage of the job applicant's salary—paid by the hiring company.

INTERNAL RECRUITING

In many large companies, the personnel office actually puts out a monthly newsletter within the company that lists new job openings. These can range from secretarial and clerical positions all the way to upper-level management positions. Employees who are interested in the new job opening are encouraged to apply, and are usually guaranteed an interview by the company's personnel department, although other applicants from outside the company are considered as well. The only stipulation in many firms is that an employee must stay at his or her present job for at least one year before applying for another one. In smaller companies where it isn't practical to have an in-house newsletter, there are other ways of getting the word around. A company bulletin board is where new job listings are usually posted.

If you have a union, your company might be bound to let union members be the first to know about job listings so that they have some advantage. Whatever the particular situation your company is in, it almost always makes sense to look within your ranks first before turning to the external market.

COLLEGE RECRUITING

Particularly when you are looking for a group of young men and women to train, one of the best places to look for new managerial talent is on the college campus. Try to establish a rapport with some of the local colleges and universities in your area. Contact the school and tell them what kind of people you are looking for. Let the school do the prescreening of applicants for you.

Whether you are looking for sales trainees or marketing managerial trainees, college campuses are always a good place to start. In addition, employing college students during their summer recess from college is also a good idea. You can use that two-month period as a sort of "trial evaluation" period for the student, to see how well he or she works within your organization.

In case you're looking for highly technical people, or individuals who have a speciality in computer training or electronics, don't overlook the various vocational training schools. Unlike people with a regular degree with a liberal arts background, these individuals have devoted their time to learning and understanding a particular vocational skill.

In addition, individuals who have served in the country's armed forces also have technical skills that they acquired while in service. Again, if you're looking for highly motivated, highly skilled employees, the armed services reentry office should be on your list of places to look.

ASK YOUR CURRENT EMPLOYEES

One of the best ways of recruiting new workers is by asking your current full-time employees. Chances are that if you set up some sort of incentive program, your workers will begin to let you know of some of their friends who might be interested in working for your company. This is a common practice in many corporations. Sometimes the incentive is a small amount of cash. If the employee brings in a qualified applicant, there is a cash bonus. If the qualified applicant does, in fact, get hired, the employee gets a little more cash. This procedure has worked well over the years, because it rewards the employee if he or she brings in only the best-qualified workers, plus it gives the employee a vested interest in how well the friend does on the job.

JOB FAIRS AND SEMINARS

When you go to conventions and seminars in your industry, that's always a good opportunity to get the word out that you're looking for qualified personnel. You don't have to publicize the fact; many times, just a few well-placed words in the right places at such affairs can produce a stream of interested applicants who are currently working for some of your competitors. This approach is popular because, like advertising in trade magazines, you know that you are going to attract people who are already familiar with the industry and with your company.

NETWORKING

One of the more recent approaches to finding good employees has developed out of a process called "networking." Basically, networking occurs in a rather spontaneous setting where several managers get together for an informal meeting, perhaps over lunch, and discuss what they are doing in their jobs and what their needs are.

Many times, these discussions will lead to one person telling another about a particular individual who might be well suited for a job opening. More often than not, these managers work in companies that are competitive with each other, but when the word of a new job opening gets around, the word tends to spread quickly. The ultimate result is that you have better access to eager and qualified personnel.

WHAT ABOUT THOSE CLASSIFIED ADVERTISEMENTS?

There's real skill involved in writing classified advertising, a skill that many managers and personnel directors overlook. You have to realize that if you place an advertisement in a newspaper, the kind of response you get depends to a large extent on just how "attractive" the position sounds.

Here are a few items to keep in mind when putting together the copy for the advertisement:

• Be upbeat. Always make the job sound as positive and as stimulating as possible. If there is anything negative, or uncertain, about the position described in your advertisement, people are not going to bother to apply.

• List the benefits, including salary range: People want to know what makes this job more attractive than the others. Let them know. Show that the benefits of the job (may) include excellent working conditions, good location, flextime, bonuses, whatever.

Let them know what kind of salary you want to pay. A salary range is all right to publish; it will help screen some of the applicants for you.

- Should it be a "blind" advertisement? A "blind" advertisement is one that doesn't list the name of your company, but rather gives a post office box number the
applicant can send a letter and résumé to.

  What's the advantage? First, it keeps your firm from
being swamped by job applicants at your door. Second,
in case you are trying to replace one of your present
employees, there's only a limited chance of embarrassing situations.

  On the other hand, many qualified people are turned
off by "blind" advertisements; they would rather know
ahead of time which company it is they are applying
to.

- Compare the following two advertisements for the same
position. Which advertisement would you respond to?

MARKETING MANAGER

**We're looking for an aggressive person who doesn't mind
working long hours. Knowledge of insurance trends
helpful; we're thinking of expanding our operation. Send
cover letter, résumé to address below. Good salary, usual
benefits.**

MARKETING MANAGER

**We're looking for that special individual who wants to-
make it to the top. If you have been watching the latest
trends in the insurance industry, and you're eager to
help us grow with a new department, please contact us
immediately.**

We're offering a salary range of $40,000 to $50,000, depending on your background. Our office is brand-new, complete with its own physical fitness room, and we're centrally located. Please send a cover letter and résumé to the address below.

Both employers are looking for the same kind of person. But the second advertisement "sounds" exciting; the first one reads like most ordinary jobs. In addition, the second one is more specific, to the point, and it helps screen applicants before they apply. It also makes the company sound youthful, energetic and eager. Again, ask yourself: Which job offer would I respond to?

MAKING CERTAIN
YOUR APPLICATION FORM
IS LEGAL

When putting together or updating your company's basic employee application form, ask yourself these questions:

- What is the general purpose of this application form?

- What am I trying to find out about this individual?

- How can I use the filled-out application to tell me more about this job candidate?

- And finally, is the application in compliance with federal laws?

If you can answer these four questions, then you're on your way to a fairly solid application form. But if you're uncertain on some of these points, keep in mind that most companies have such poorly written application forms that errors are more common than you think.

First of all, realize right from the start that an application form is a company instrument you can utilize to help screen applicants. Yes, it's true that the candidate might appear to be charming, well mannered, articulate, and considerate, but his or her filled-in application form is your first definitive document of who this person is, what he or she can do, and whether he or she might make a good employee.

In other words, from your application form, you should be able to find out a little bit about the individuals' work history. What kind of jobs they have had. For how long. Who they have worked for. And what kind of salary.

Sometimes, when going over the chronology of an individual's work history, you might detect certain gaps in time. That's always worth asking about, as in, "I notice you don't account for the months from January 1982 to September 1982. . . . Can you tell me what you were doing then?"

When you ask for references or recommendations, note if the job applicant puts down any former supervisors from previously held jobs. If he or she has done good work elsewhere, recommendations should flow freely.

And, looking at the individual's job history, has he or she held a particular job for a long period of time, or jumped from one to another after a matter of only a few months? And what about those jobs—have they been in the same line of work, or are they scattered all over the lot?

These are just a few of the items you can detect from a full and comprehensive application form. True, such a form may take a little while to fill out completely, but those extra few minutes before you even interview the applicant might save you a great deal of trouble later on.

To illustrate what a good sample job application form looks like, take a look at Exhibit 16. Granted, this is generalized in scope, and for a particular position, you may want to tailor the application accordingly; but on an overall basis, here's a good start.

EXHIBIT 16

Sample Application Form

ABC COMPANY
Sample Employment Application Form

Please complete all the questions on this form truthfully because this company uses this data to screen candidates for jobs and because the information you provide may be checked for accuracy with previous employers.

Personal Data

Last name (print)_____First_____Middle_____

Today's Date_____Social Security No._____

Home address_____Telephone No._____

Have you worked for ABC Company before?_____

☐ Yes ☐ No

Where?_____When?_____

Are you a U.S. citizen?_____

If not, enter alien registration no._____

☐ Yes ☐ No

Age (check one) ☐ under 18 ☐ between 18–70 ☐ over 70

Are you applying for a:

☐ full-time position   ☐ part-time position

Outside interests (clubs, hobbies, sports, community activities, etc.)

_____

_____

Work Experience

Last job (or present position)_____

Name and address of employer_____

Date started_____Date left_____

Description of duties at last job_____

Beginning salary_____Final salary_____

What did you like best about the job?_____

_____

_____

What did you like least about the job?_____

_____

Reasons for leaving_____

_____

Second last job_____

Name and address of employer_____

Description of duties at that job_____

Beginning salary_____Final salary_____

What did you like best about that job?_____

_____

What did you like least about it?_____

_____

Reasons for leaving_____

_____

Third last job_____

Name and address of employer_____

Description of duties at that job_____

_____

Beginning salary_____Final salary_____

What did you like best about that job?_____

_____

What did you like least about it?_____

_____

Reasons for leaving_____

Educational Background

Name of school_____

Location_____Did you graduate?_____

Grade School_____

High School_____

Trade School_____

College_____

Graduate School_____

Military experience: Did you serve in the U.S. Armed Forces? If yes, please explain when and where. Indicate what kind of discharge you received.

In the event of employment, I understand that false or misleading information given on my application or interview(s) may result in discharge. I understand also that I am required to abide by all rules and regulations of the company.

_____

Signature of applicant   Date

ONE LITTLE POSTSCRIPT...

As you have probably heard, there is a new trend of lawsuits popping up over the United States regarding wrongful discharge of employees. In a nutshell, employees who feel that they have been wrongfully dismissed from their jobs or somehow cheated by an employer after certain "promises" were made to that employee have brought suit in state courts and—much to the chargrin of companies—have won more often than not.

Because of this growing surge of lawsuits, some companies are now beginning to insert lengthy postscripts at the end of the employee's application form in order to protect and ensure the company's rights. The following addendum is a sample of such an employer "protection" clause. Take the time to read it, and then decide if you want to add it to your company's application form.

I certify that the information contained in this application is correct to the best of my knowledge and understand that falsification of this information is grounds for refusal to hire or, if hired, dismissal. I authorize any of the persons or organizations referenced in this application to give you any and all information concerning my previous employment, education, or any other information they might have, personal or otherwise, with regard to any of the subjects covered by this application and release all such parties from all liability for any damage that may result from furnishing such information to you. I authorize you to request and receive such information. In consideration for my employment and my being considered for employment by your company, I agree to conform to the rules and regulations of the company and acknowledge that these rules and regulations may be changed, interpreted, withdrawn, or added to by your company at any time, at the company's sole option and without any prior notice to me. I further acknowledge that my employment may be terminated, and any offer of employment, if such is made, may be withdrawn, with or without cause, and with or without prior notice, at any time, at the option of the company or myself. I understand that no representative of the company has any authority to enter into any agreement for employment for any specified period of time, or make some other personnel move, either prior to commencement of employment or after I have become employed, or to assure any benefits or terms and conditions of employment, or make any agreement contrary to the foregoing. I acknowledge that I have been advised that this application will remain active for no more than 90 days from the date it was made.

Application Forms — Legal and Illegal Questions

SUBJECT	LAWFUL	UNLAWFUL
Race		Any inquiry into one's race or color

SUBJECT	**LAWFUL**	**UNLAWFUL**
Religion or creed		Any inquiry into religious denomination, religious holidays observed. Applicant may not be told "This is a (Catholic, Jewish, etc.) organization."
National origin		Any inquiry into one's lineage, nationality, or of his/her parents or spouse. Can't ask what is their "native" tongue.
Sex		Can't ask one whether they prefer to be called Mr., Mrs., Miss, or Ms.
Marital status		Can't ask whether they're married, divorced, or separated. Can't ask for any data regarding spouse. Can't ask for ages of children.
Family planning		Can't ask about plans for family.
Age	Are you between 18–70 years of age? If not, how old are you?	Can't ask: How old are you? Can't ask for date of birth.
Arrest record	Have you ever been convicted of a crime? Give details	Have you ever been arrested?
Birthplace		Can't ask applicant's birthplace, or birthplace of applicant's parents or spouse.

SUBJECT	LAWFUL	UNLAWFUL
Disability	Do you have any physical or mental impairments which might interfere with your ability to perform your job duties?	Do you have a disability? Have you ever been treated for any of the following diseases?
Name	Have you ever worked for this company under a different name?	Can't ask maiden name of a married woman.
Photograph		Can't ask an applicant to affix a photo with application form
Citizenship	Are you a citizen of the U.S.?	Can't ask: Of what country are you a citizen?
		Whether applicant is naturalized or native-born citizen.
		Can't ask for naturalization papers.
Language	Inquiry into languages spoken and written fluently.	What is your native language?
Education	Inquiry into applicant's academic, vocational, or professional schooling.	
Experience	Inquiry into work experience.	
Relatives	Name of applicant's relatives, other than spouse, already employed by company	Can't ask for names, ages, addresses of applicant's spouse, children, relatives not employed by company

SUBJECT	**LAWFUL**	**UNLAWFUL**
Notice in case of emergency		Can't ask for such information
Military experience	Inquiry into applicant's military experience in the U.S. Armed Forces and his/her branch in service	

After you have written your final version of your company's application form, take the time to send a copy of it over to your legal counsel to make certain you have not interfered with any EEO laws; it's the kind of precaution that can only save you legal headaches in the future.

PART II

EMPLOYEE TESTING

INTRODUCTION

Testing adds an important objective ingredient to the employee selection process which is often highly subjective. Testing can be used not only as an efficient measurement of people's intelligence, aptitude and skills, but as a reliable predictor of future performance.

The personnel department at your firm may already have a testing program in place for certain jobs. Or, your current position may not lend itself to the profitable use of testing for choosing future employees. Nevertheless, you should have a firm grasp of what testing can—and cannot—do for your company and your department. It will prove a valuable resource at some point in your management career.

The concept of testing has had its ups and downs from the standpoint of popularity over the last few years. The concerns of EEO have pushed it out of the mainstream of some companies' selection process. And experts agree that it should not be used as the sole criterion for candidate selection.

But today's progressive managers recognize testing for what it can do for them. How it can provide them with better subordinates. How it can upgrade the selection process throughout their companies. How it can create a more productive organization. And how it can help them stand out from their colleagues as innovators in the eyes of upper-level management.

This section explains how you can use tests most profitably at your company, where they can be best applied, and how to analyze and validate them.

It also provides some examples of what you'll find when you look into specific tests and leads you into the Appendices, with some capsule comments on two companies in the forefront of testing today.

The two testing Appendices (A and B) will show you the key to probing reference libraries on tests and where to look for answers to specific questions you may have.

While not every test or publisher will be able to satisfy your specific needs, the breadth of information should enable you or anyone else in your company charged with employee selection to carry out that task in a more professional and responsible manner.

As in all phases of employee selection today, the EEO ingredient in testing must not be overlooked. You'll find some general guidelines in this section on how to integrate EEO considerations into any testing with which you may become involved. You'll also find specific information on special testing services from the federal government, and on a national testing library that should provide the answers to almost any question you might have on individual tests.

SOME BACKGROUND
ON TESTING AND EEO

Aptitude tests have long been used as reliable mechanisms for measuring aptitudes in the plant and office setting. In fact, aptitude tests in most cases represent a far more accurate tool for measuring certain ability factors than does any other device. No matter how proficient you are as an interviewer, tests of mental ability, verbal ability, numerical ability, mechanical comprehension, clerical aptitude, and manual dexterity may provide more valid results than can be obtained by means of the interview.

Some companies have mistakenly and needlessly eliminated testing because they believe this is no longer possible under EEO regulations. Nothing could be further from the truth. EEO regulations simply require that there be a positive relationship between the test and performance on the job. If such a relationship cannot be demonstrated, you shouldn't be using that test anyway, since it yields no helpful selection information.

The development and validation of employment tests for a specific plant or office situation may require an expertise that you or your personnel department do not have. In that case, you should seek out a professional in this area.

Transportability, or what some people call validity generalization, is a characteristic that makes possible a much wider utilization of aptitude tests than you might have expected. The term simply means that if a test can be shown to be valid for a given job in one plant situation, that same test can be assumed to be valid for that specific job in other plant locations.

USING THE U.S. EMPLOYMENT SERVICE

If your company does not wish to take the time or incur the expense of developing its own employment tests, there is an alternative. The U.S. Employment Service (USES) of the U.S. Department of Labor has developed a General Aptitude Test Battery (GATB) which has been in use since 1947 by state employment service offices. The existence of GATB and its application by individual states is not widely known or understood in industry. Yet, any company, large or small, can ask its state employment service to administer appropriate tests as part of its selection procedure.

The GATB measures nine aptitudes.

- general learning ability (vocabulary and arithmetic reasoning);

- verbal aptitude (vocabulary);

- numerical aptitude (computation and arithmetic reasoning);

- spatial aptitude (three-dimensional space perception);
- form perception (tool matching and form matching);
- clerical perception (name comparison);
- motor coordination (mark making);
- finger dexterity (placing and turning).

Here is a condensed description of the nine tests of GATB extracted from federal government literature:

G (general learning ability)—Ability to "catch on" or understand instructions and underlying principles; ability to reason and make judgments. Closely related to doing well in school.

V (verbal aptitude)—Ability to understand the meaning of words and use them effectively; ability to comprehend language, to understand relationships between words, and to understand the meanings of whole sentences and paragraphs.

N (numerical aptitude)—Ability to perform arithmetic operations quickly and accurately.

S (spatial aptitude)—Ability to think visually of geometric forms and to comprehend two-dimensional representations of three-dimensional objects; ability to recognize relationships resulting from the movements of objects in space.

P (form perception)—Ability to perceive pertinent details in objects or in pictorial or graph material; ability to make visual comparison and discrimination and see slight differences in shapes and shadings of figures and widths and lengths of lines.

Q (clerical perception)—Ability to perceive pertinent details in verbal or tabular material; ability to observe differences in copy, to proofread words and numbers, and to avoid perceptual errors in arithmetic computation. A measure of speed of perception which is required in many industrial jobs even when the job does not have verbal or numerical content.

K (motor coordination)—Ability to coordinate eyes with hands or fingers rapidly and accurately and to make precise movements with speed; ability to make a movement response accurately and swiftly.

F (finger dexterity)—Ability to move the fingers and manipulate small objects with the fingers, rapidly or accurately.

M (manual dexterity)—Ability to move the hands easily and skillfully; ability to work with the hands in placing and turning motions.

Over the years, norms have been developed for each test which makes it possible to determine how well an applicant scores in comparison with the population upon which the test was standarized. Test norms for specific occupations also provide minimum-aptitude scores, the score below which the individual is not likely to be at all successful on the job.

Because the GATB was developed by the federal government, it is available as previously stated in all the various state employment offices. To take advantage of this testing service, you must contact your state employment service; they will administer the appropriate tests for the specific job involved.

QUESTIONS TO ASK
ABOUT YOUR OWN TESTS

If you've decided to use tests, or you already have them as part of your selection system, the following is a checklist of questions you should ask about them in relation to EEO standards:

1. Compare the tests and the jobs for which they are designed. Are the tests specifically related to the appropriate qualifications for the job?

2. Who designed the tests, a professional test-publishing firm or someone in-house at the company?

3. If in-house, were the tests validated by a professional on the basis of specific job-related criteria?

4. If in-house, what were the qualifications of the person who designed it?

5. Where was the test first designed? Has it been updated? What changes were incorporated?

6. Who administers the tests at your firm? The personnel director? An outside consultant? You?

7. What are the qualifications of that administrator? And who has responsibility to oversee his or her efforts?

8. Have you checked that the population used in validating your test included a representative sample of minorities?

9. Is there a continuous program of revalidation?

10. Have passing scores been reevaluated and updated? When?

11. Have any applicants who failed a test been hired? Is there information on why and when it happened?

12. Can failed applicants be retested? How and why?

13. Have the tests been applied to current employees as well? What is the standard reaction if they fail?

14. Do all applicants take the same test? If not, why?

15. Are all tests administered uniformly? Are they graded consistently?

16. What are your practices on retaining the results of the tests?

TESTING:
A VITAL COMPONENT IN THE
EMPLOYEE SELECTION PROCESS

Psychological and physical tests are useful in both evaluating potential employees and judging the capability of current ones. In the process of selecting new employees, tests can help:

1. Forecast success or failure on the job.

2. Eliminate subjective judgments of applicants.

3. Cut costs by eliminating candidates slated for failure.

4. Select people who can work effectively in your company's particular environments.

5. Identify and eliminate candidates whose principle talent is doing well in job interviews.

JOBS BEST SUITED FOR TESTING

The type of job involved plays a significant role in determining the value and necessity of testing in employee selection. Experts in the field of business and industry have developed tests and established criteria for a significant percentage of today's job market.

Managers have found that tests are most aptly employed to evaluate jobs:

- in which the line between acceptance and unacceptable performance is agreed upon by all management people involved;

- in groups that require essentially the same skills, so that the number of tests to be given does not become burdensome;

- for which the labor pool available is large enough for management to have a real opportunity to choose among applicants;

- for which required skills can be identified and described;

- whose criteria remain constant over time;

- for which recruitment, training, and turnover costs are high;

- where the selection procedure is comprehensive, and tests are not the only tool employed.

Even when one or more of the foregoing conditions exist, managers have found that not every applicant is always a candidate for testing. For example, a welder who has a verifiable and satisfactory employment history in similar jobs probably doesn't need a performance test. And an experienced executive secretary coming from a recent similar position would not always be given typing and shorthand tests.

Evaluating Current Employees

For people already on the job, tests can help you to:

- measure whether present employees are properly matched to their jobs;

- uncover potential for improving performance;

- objectively select candidates for promotion;

- compare performance before and after training;

- make possible written definitions of job requirements;

- assist in the creation of training programs;

- reduce costs of poor performance;

- create objective standards and reduce favoritism;

- and raise employee morale by instituting objective performance measures.

ADVANTAGES OF TESTING

The major advantage of psychological tests in the selection process is that they tend to be objective. Every candidate has the same questions to answer or the same tasks to perform. Ideally, each person taking the test is given exactly the same amount of time in which to complete it. The physical environment should also be similar for each applicant—the noise level, lighting, nonintrusion of outsiders, temperature. Then the chances of impartial interpretation and grading of the test results are high. This kind of objectivity afforded by tests is important to the selection task.

A second major advantage of tests is that they provide immediate quantitative measures of intelligence, skills and aptitudes. Assessing an individual's intelligence from manner or appearance, or even from a lengthy interview, is usually imprecise. But an hour-long intelligence test can give a reliable measure of an individual's intelligence, and also make it possible to compare that person's intelligence level to those of other applicants. Similarly, you can determine the accuracy of an applicant's claims of skill levels in such areas as clerical, mechanical, etc., when those assertions cannot be easily verified with previous employers.

PROBLEMS IN USING TESTS

Many employers, dismayed by mediocre results in their companies' hiring decisions, turn to testing as a guaranteed solution to all their problems. They view the numerical rating attached to each applicant's intelligence, skill or aptitude as a sure sign of what the future holds for that person. Unfortunately, that is not always the case. In addition, an employer cannot assume that, if one candidate outscores another by a few points on a given test, he or she is definitely the most qualified for the job. A difference of a few points on many tests does not indicate significant variations in quality.

Managers must also be aware of job characteristics and requirements. There are positions in which a person with a lower score is better qualified than one with a higher score. For example, a simple key-punch operation is quickly mastered by a person who scores well on an intelligence test. But the job may just as quickly induce boredom in that individual, and chances are that person will not stay long on the job. An individual with a lower score, on the other hand, may take longer to learn the operation and cost more to train. But once that individual has mastered the job, he or she is much more likely to stay. The reduced turnover costs will more than make up for the increased cost of training.

Perhaps the greatest danger faced by the employer is specific test selection. The name of a test often makes it appear as if it applies to a given job, whereas experience eventually proves that it does not. For example, many clerical-aptitude tests have been proven to be accurate measures of the skills needed in accounting clerks. Those same tests might seem appropriate for bank tellers. But the differences between the two jobs in some cases have proven so wide that the tests have no predictive value at all on how people taking it would fare as bank tellers. An employer should make certain that the test selected has been validated as a successful predictor by people performing that exact job.

HOW EMPLOYEES
USE TESTING FOR BEST
RESULTS

A test can assemble objective data about an individual that other selection techniques cannot. That information predicting an applicant's performance, however, should not be the sole—or even the final—criterion of whether or not to hire. The manager should make that decision on the basis of a series of data collected by several methods, such as personal interviews (see Part III), reference checks, self-statements, and consideration of the individual's history.

The test itself will measure the applicants' skill or predict their performance in areas which are directly related to the criteria of the job to be filled (see Part I). Those criteria must be specific and quantifiable. Once they have been established, the skills necessary to achieve those criteria can also be established. On the next page is an example.

The performance skills listed opposite each job criterion are only two of many it would take to successfully match the corresponding job criterion.

Job Criterion	Two Applicable Performance Skills
Achieve specific dollar sales level per month.	Gains rapport with people easily. Asks for orders assertively.
Produce certain numbers of units per hour.	Coordinates eye, hand, and foot motions. Learns new machine operations rapidly.
Set up machine in set amount of time.	Analyzes mechanical movements accurately. Concentrates well, accelerating task completion.

A REAL-LIFE EXAMPLE OF TEST USE

Sales aptitude has traditionally been a difficult area in which to forecast success. One method that has proven useful for such assessment is a battery of tests which measures such qualities as resourcefulness, decisiveness, stress endurance, general intelligence, social judgment, etc.

An applicant's score on all these tests is compiled in a form like the one shown in Exhibit 17, and interpreted by a professional psychologist. The manager doing the hiring thus receives an individualized picture of the person's probable day-to-day behavior on the job.

EXHIBIT 17

A Psychological Data Collection Form

PSYCHOLOGICAL INFORMATION

Name_____   Date:_____

Company:_____   Term:_____

Administrator:_____   Location:_____

	DESIR-ABLE	ACCEPT-ABLE	UNAC-CEPTABLE
GENERAL INTELLECT:			
Mental Capacity—Trainability			
Mental Alertness—Receptivity			
PERSONALITY STRUCTURE:			
Ego Strength			
Emotional Stability			
Self-Assurance/Confidence			
Take-Charge Capacity			
Self-Sufficiency			
Vitality			
Overall Sociability			

	DESIR-ABLE	**ACCEPT-ABLE**	**UNAC-CEPTABLE**
SALES APTITUDE:			
Sales/Persuasive Interest			
Sales Judgment			
SOCIAL JUDGMENT:			
Tact and Diplomacy			
Interpersonal Feeling			
ADJUSTMENT:			
Career/Vocational Planning			
Ambition/Achieve-ment Motivation			
Persistence			
Systematic Behavior			
OTHER INTERESTS:			
Sports			
Entertainer			
Teacher			
Personnel Counselor			
OTHER FACTORS:			
Money as Incentive			
Sensitivity to Criticism			
Strong-Willed			

Specific Testing Benefits

According to those who currently use testing as part of the screening process, this type of interpretation offers the manager doing the hiring a number of specific benefits not otherwise available. No single rating on a test like the one pictured here is considered alone. The interpreting psychologist considers the profile as a whole, rather than individual items.

The actual job for which a candidate is being considered is also a factor. An individual applying for a sales job working out of headquarters with a manager close at hand would not necessarily be damaged by a low score on self-sufficiency. However, a person with a similar score being considered for a sales job with the same company, selling the same product, but working out of an outlying office with no manager in charge, would be damaged.

The numbers themselves are not *scores*. They are *percentiles* based on norms established by years of testing experience with new salespeople in a number of major corporations. The sales records achieved over the years are then compared with test scores recorded at the beginning of their careers.

The population on which the norms are based is all *successful* salespeople. Therefore, a fairly low percentile ranking in such a group is not as disqualifying as a low standing in the population as a whole.

First, such interpretations *create a basis for comparison to employees already working for the company*. "After you've been using the tests for a few years, you have a data bank that's very useful," says the president of a construction materials firm. "I can compare applicants' test results with those of people who have been successful with my firm. And I can compare them with people whom I hired because

I expected them to be successful, but who weren't. Thus, I'm able to sharpen my own awareness of the qualities necessary for success in this business, while at the same time spotting possible areas of weakness."

Second, *professional assessments can flash warning lights about even promising candidates.* "Sometimes the professional's analysis of test results is a surprise," says the sales manager of an accounting machine manufacturer. "He might tell us that a person who displayed apparent confidence in the interview turns out, according to the tests, to be someone who feels initially insecure in new situations. That would certainly make us hesitant to hire him or her for a new job. "One thing we can do with such new persons is to keep them off straight commission. For an extended period, we put them on mostly salary plus a small bonus arrangement. After they've built up some real confidence in their ability to make it with us, the commission deal poses no psychological hazard. But if we were to do it too early, it could be a disaster."

Third, *without professional help, high performance skill-test results may be applied incorrectly.* Here's how the head of a major social agency found that to be true:

> We decided that in an environment such as ours, with a high percentage of professionals on the staff and a very high intelligence level in the office, everyone should be very bright. That included our typist-receptionists, who were the first contact our clients had with the agency, and therefore very important.
>
> In practice, however, each of the ten typists got to serve as a receptionist only one day every two weeks, since we rotated the job. The other nine days they did straight typing. Soon they began to leave in very rapid succession as they found their duties insufficiently demanding in relation to their intelligence.

We changed our system by assigning one highly intelligent typist to full-time receptionist duty, a job varied enough to keep her challenged. As for the other typing jobs, we filled them with applicants whose scores were between 100 and 105 on the general intelligence test we use, well below the 130 that had been our previous minimum.

TEN QUESTIONS TO ASK ABOUT YOUR OWN TEST PROCEDURE

A reliable testing program involves several important factors, including:

- An analysis of the knowledge, skills and other requirements that promote successful performance in a specific job.

- A decision as to which of those performance skills can be measured by a test.

- The selection of an appropriate test of those skills that has been validated by people performing the same job.

For a testing program to meet those criteria, and contribute to the overall goal of higher employee achievement, you should make sure you can answer the following ten questions affirmatively.

1. Are the tests used to screen applicants specifically related to the jobs for which they are applying?

2. Is there evidence of job-relatedness that proves that the tests are valid?

3. Are applicants given instructions for taking tests, if they are unfamiliar with the process?

4. Are the tests being administered by a qualified person in a comfortable environment?

5. Are the tests always scored accurately, consistently and fairly?

6. Are applicants retested if they were originally tested under unfavorable conditions?

7. Are test results only one factor in the hiring decision?

8. Are employees ever retested as a measure of progress on the job?

9. Are test results a significant part of promotion decisions?

10. Does the company test and retest employees who have varying degrees of success in their job performance in order to determine test validity and reliability?

MEASURES OF INTELLIGENCE

What is intelligence? Definitions range form problem-solving ability to rapid-learning ability to common sense to dealing effectively with one's world. Even the experts, the psychologists, have not agreed upon a set definition. Those professionals enumerate such concepts as the ability to use good judgment, to comprehend new concepts, to reason well, to think abstractly, to deal well with language, to understand spatial relationships, and to remember well. Some psychologists claim that these all add up to a single general intelligence that they call the "G factor." Others maintain that there are several factors, and that each individual does not necessarily possess equal amounts of each.

BACKGROUND TO INTELLIGENCE TESTING

The challenge, then, still exists today: Create a test to measure a quality with certifiable definition. The first intelligence tests were devised by Alfred Binet, a French psychologist; he created a test to predict the success or failure of students in the public schools of Paris. He observed the tasks and problems which the majority of local schoolchildren could perform and solve at various ages. He then set up increasingly difficult levels of problems within each task category—each level corresponding to a specific age—and the children were scored on the levels they achieved. The tests did predict school success, correctly categorizing the children who took them, on a numerical scale, from "bright" to "dull." Thus, without being sure of exactly what was being tested, Binet nonetheless devised a method to forecast how the children would fare in school.

Still without a solid definition of what was being tested, the U.S. Army's Alpha and Beta tests categorized draftees—correctly, experience showed—on their ability to master military tasks. Right through the 1940s the same kinds of general intelligence tests continued to discriminate successfully among the very bright, bright, average and below average people who took them. They predicted who would do well, and who would not. Since that time, however, psychologists and business executives gradually have recognized that for many job categories a general intelligence test is less useful than a test of a specific ability.

Most modern professionals acknowledge five basic components as being identifiable and, more importantly, the most frequently needed abilities *on the job*. The five are:

- verbal ability
- numerical ability
- perceptual speed
- spatial ability
- reasoning ability

Individual tests have been developed to test each of these mental abilities, although some general intelligence tests are still used.

FIVE MAIN ON-THE-JOB TESTS

Tests of verbal ability involve an individual's ability to use language or words as tools in thinking, communicating, and planning ahead. This ability is critical at the managerial level, as well as for responsibilities in copywriting, technical jobs, and sales jobs. Verbal ability is usually measured by vocabulary tests, such as synonym-antonym problems, or multiple-choice questions in which the person being tested must select a word that matches another word in meaning. Other tests present a passage to read, and then require the reader to answer questions—usually multiple choice—relating to the passage.

Tests of numerical ability help determine a person's ability to deal with the four basic arithmetic functions: addition, subtraction, multiplication and division. Depending on the level of job being tested for—for instance, bank clerk or engineer—the problems given can range from fairly simple to very difficult. The test may require, for example, the use of decimals, or positive and negative numbers. When the level of difficulty gets too high, reasoning ability rather than numerical ability becomes tested. That hazard can also arise when the problems are stated in words rather than in numerals.

Tests of perceptual speed measure the rate at which a person perceives detailed similarities or differences in familiar words or objects. Usually pairs of words, names, numbers, or other common symbols are presented, and the subject is asked whether the two members of each pair are alike or not alike. Clerical work in particular demands this kind of rapid perception.

Tests of spatial ability assess the individual's capacity to visualize figures in space and their relationships to one another. Sometimes two almost identical figures are depicted, and the person being tested must detect whether one is actually the mirror image of the other. Or a figure in three dimensions may be shown next to a flat drawing with dotted lines. If the drawing is folded along those lines, it may or may not re-create that original figure. Engineers, designers, and mechanics require this ability.

Tests of reasoning ability deal with the capability to handle logically a variety of materials, words, figures, or abstractions. A typical problem offers a set of four "problem figures," which represent a series of positions. The subject must choose one of five "answer figures" as the one that logically comes next. It is an ability fundamental to a decision-making responsibility, and applies to administrators, salespeople, teachers, and especially managers.

EXAMPLES OF INTELLIGENCE TESTS

Many specific intelligence tests are designed to analyze one or more of the five previously mentioned main business-oriented capacities. Among the most common are:

- *SRA verbal form* is group-administered and tests verbal, numerical and reasoning ability. It yields three scores: verbal, numerical, and total. (See Chapter 20 for more.)

- *California Test of Mental Maturity, long form, level 5*, is group-administered and separately scores logical reasoning, spatial relationships, numerical reasoning, verbal concepts, memory, and a number of other aspects of mental ability.

- *Academic–Aptitude Test–Verbal Intelligence* is group-administered and designed to predict the abilities of an applicant in a job that requires independent judgment or mental alertness. Factors tested include general information, mental alertness, and comprehension of relationships.

- *Differential Aptitude Tests* is a group-administered battery that scores verbal reasoning, numerical ability, abstract reasoning, spatial relationships, mechanical reasoning, clerical speed and accuracy, spelling, and language usage.

- *Otis Quick-Scoring Mental Ability Tests* are group-administered tests yielding a simple score covering vocabulary, perceptual features, arithmetic, and reasoning.

- *Wonderlic Personnel Test* is group-administered and yields a single score based on verbal, arithmetic, and perceptual questions.

- *Wechsler Adult Intelligence Scale* is individually administered and provides eleven scores, divided into two groups. The verbal group includes general information, comprehension, arithmetic, perception of similarities, number recall, and vocabulary. The performance group includes responding to abstract symbols, completing incomplete pictures, arranging blocks in a design, arranging pictures to tell a story, and object assembly.

- *Stanford-Binet Intelligence Scale* is individually administered from early childhood to the adult level. The adult test offers a single score based on vocabulary, reasoning, general information, spatial ability, numerical ability, and certain performance items.

VALUE OF TESTS
FOR EMPLOYERS

An employer realizes three main practical advantages by using tests of mental ability. One lies in screening a surplus of applicants. Every job requires a certain level of intelligence. When the number of applicants is greater than the number of openings available, you can use an intelligence test to screen out a large number of the excess group faster and more economically than through individual interviews. A second advantage exists in screening applicants for proper level. For some jobs, high intelligence can be as much of a negative factor as too-low mental ability is in others. An intelligence test allows you to know that you are interviewing people whose mental ability is appropriate for the job. The third major plus is selecting people for promotion as well as for entry. Testing is but one factor in such decisions. But the fact is that people who do best in these tests are, by and large, the intelligent people who lead the way in business. So a tool that helps choose those who are promotable today, as well as those who are likely to be successful, is a powerful one.

Testing can also prove valuable to you as a corporate manager on the move. The ability to understand where testing works best and how to utilize a testing program is a key management skill. It will set you apart from the rest of the management crowd. As you hone your interpretive skills in testing, you'll become more aware of what works best—and what doesn't—at your company. You'll contribute more to the successful progression into the future of its operations. And you'll become known as a multitalented individual who has worked to extend your skills into crucial aspects of the company's personnel activities.

MEASURES OF PROFICIENCIES, SKILLS AND JOB INFORMATION

The ultimate goal of your hiring decision is to add new value to your company's production that would not have been there without that new employee. Testing applicants for the skills they possess offers a valuable insight into who will become most successful. This measurement involves testing people for what they already know how to do—job skill—rather than for what they are suited to do—job aptitude. Since an applicant's perception of what he or she can accomplish is often at variance with reality, it becomes important to test skills and knowledge as a way of establishing actual skill levels.

UTILIZING SKILLS TESTING

Skills testing involves both standard questionnaire techniques and actual performance on the equipment to be used, or an adaptation of it. Many tests combine the two methods.

Managers seeking employees realize that a person's knowledge about a job is not a guarantee that he or she can actually perform its requirements. When the written test is not a duplicate of the job itself, it becomes a screening device, one that experience indicates is a very good predictor.

Skills testing achieves two distinct benefits for the employer. First, it can rank candidates from "most qualified" to "least qualified" and measure them against criteria the employer has set up. Those criteria can be used to select from among experienced job applicants, as well as apprentices who have completed trade courses. You can even apply them in determining which of your people will contribute most to the company's productivity by promotion or transfer.

Second, such skills-performance tests can uncover training needs and help a firm develop a training program. And repeating the test—usually in a slightly different form—can measure the effectiveness of the training program after its completion.

A WIDE RANGE OF SPECIALIZED TESTS

Many executives today use mechanical trade tests which were originated at Purdue University's highly rated engineering school. Among the most popular are:

1. *Purdue Trade Information Test in Engine Operation.* Covers operating information well known to any qualified engine-lathe operator, known to a lesser extent among people who have had good vocational instruction in this area.

2. *Purdue Industrial Mathematics Test.* Measures the un-

derstanding of arithmetic and the ability to perform the basic computations required of people in a variety of skilled trades, and for such tasks as setup, layout, maintenance, and design.

3. *Purdue Trade Information Test in Welding.* Tests just how much experience an applicant for a welder's job possesses. It is also used as a final examination for students in vocational and other trade schools.

4. *Purdue Creativity Test.* Assesses creativity in engineering and helps pinpoint design engineers who have the capacity to produce creative work. The test also identifies research and development engineers with a propensity for developing new ideas.

Other Widely Used Tests

The Bennett Mechanical Comprehension Test is one of the most widely used tests of mechanical aptitude. It has also been used successfully for the selection of engineers, and the evaluation of academic knowledge acquired in physics courses at both high school and college levels. It is basically a test of mechanical principles, and requires no mathematical computations. Because it is relatively nonverbal, hiring managers find it especially useful in jobs where verbal skills are not necessary.

One question shows two men walking, one in front of the other. They are carrying a single board which has a heavy weight hanging from its middle. The man in front has much more of the board projecting forward of his shoulder than the man behind has to the rear of his shoulder. As a result, the weight hangs almost directly in back of the front man, and well forward of the rear man. The question: Which man carries more weight? Another illustration depicts a bus, seen from the side. Arrows point to three seats. One is halfway between the front and rear wheels, the second is directly over the rear wheels, and the third is in the back row of the bus, behind the rear wheels. The question: Which is the seat where a passenger will get the smoothest ride?

The Revised Minnesota Paper Form Board Test is another well-known test that includes both aptitude and trade testing. It requires the applicant to visualize the assembly of two-dimensional geometric shapes into a whole design, thus assuring the ability to visualize and manipulate objects in space. The problems range from the very simple to the very complex. It is an excellent test of the abilities required in drafting, engineering, inspection, and power sewing-machine operation, among others.

Mechanical Manipulation Tests

Experts use a number of relatively simple—though not easy—tests that require the applicant to perform mechanical tasks. Two of the foremost are:

- *Hand-Tool Dexterity Test.* On the left-hand upright of a wooden frame approximately 9″ × 9″ × 18″ are mounted twelve bolts—four in each of three sizes. The applicant must take apart the twelve fastenings according to a prescribed sequence and reassemble the nuts, washers, and bolts in the right-hand upright. The score is the time required. This is a useful selection test for aircraft and auto mechanics, machine adjusters, and maintenance mechanics.

- *Crawford Small Parts Dexterity Test.* This is a measure of fine eye-hand coordination. The prospect uses tweezers to insert small pins in close-fitting holes in a plate, and to place small collars over the protruding pins. Also, the person must place small screws in threaded holes in a plate, and screw them down with a screwdriver until they drop through the plate into a metal dish below.

ASSESSING CLERICAL SKILLS

For the employer with jobs demanding the ability to handle information in the form of numbers and words, speed and accuracy are important in filing, verifying, checking, tabulating, summarizing, and transmitting that data. Among the most popular tests which measure abilities in spelling, arithmetic computation, reasoning, memory for oral instructions, copying and vocabulary are:

(1) the Minnesota Clerical Test,

(2) the Purdue Clerical Adaptability Test,

(3) the General Clerical Test,

(4) the Hay Aptitude Test Battery,

(5) the PSI Basic Skills Test for Industry, and

(6) Office Skills Tests.

Here are some typical questions found on clerical skills tests:

Reading comprehension: Mark has been asked to fix the photocopy machines on the fourth and seventh floors before he does his routine work. He should fix the light fixture that is out on the third floor first, however, since there have been a number of complaints about this already. Which of the following should Mark do first?

- Fix the photocopy machine on the fourth floor.
- Fix the photocopy machine on the seventh floor.
- Do his routine assignments.
- Fix the light fixture on the third floor.
- Fix the light fixture on the fourth floor.

Spelling: Please send me your_____by Friday.

- repplie
- replie
- repily
- repley
- reply

Arithmetic: Compute the following.

$\begin{array}{r} 61 \\ +\ 24 \\ \hline \end{array}$	• 70 ¾	• 2
	• 74 − ¼	• 1
	• 75	• ½
	• 84	• ¼
	• 85	• ³⁄₁₆

A special return envelope is	•	$.79
purchased by a city agency for	•	$7.90
$79.00 per thousand. How much	•	$79.00
would ten thousand envelopes	•	$790.00
cost?	•	$7,900.00

Judging stenographic ability

One of the most useful tests of stenographic ability is the Seashore-Bennett Stenographic Proficiency Test. It dictates a series of five commercial letters in a typical business voice on a tape or cassette.

Two are short and slowly dictated, two are medium in length and average in speed, and one is long and dictated rapidly. Another test employed by many managers is the Blackstone Stenographic Proficiency Test.

All these proficiency tests have one primary purpose— to assist the employer in that most difficult of tasks, predicting success on the job. These are probably the types of tests you'd find most useful in your current position. It is important to recognize not only their usefulness, however.

Many managers and even upper-level executives feel that testing clerical personnel is a waste of their time. Their testing becomes sloppy and haphazard. Then they complain when turnover is high and mistakes abound. By using standardized tests, you can avoid the biggest problems in this regard. If your personnel people do this for you, all the better.

But you know best what the job under you entails. The more you know about this type of testing—in fact, all testing—the more guidance you can give when applicants are being tested for your areas. And the fewer headaches you'll suffer later.

14

MEASURES
OF APTITUDE

Ideally, every occupational match should result in using the individual's finest talents to their maximum, while giving a company the most effective possible employee. Testing for applicants' talents and aptitudes, while it cannot guarantee achievement of that ideal, moves the prospective employer—you—closer to the realization than random hiring does.

Another reason to utilize such testing is that not all random matches between person and job are even reasonably successful. An occasional one is perfect, but many turn out to be expensive mistakes. Considerable costs fall on the organization in loss of time and efficiency, spoiled materials, alienated customers, and so forth. Both sides lose in such an unproductive arrangement, since the employee who was placed incorrectly can never recover the years he or she may have wasted. Therein lies the value of aptitude testing.

SKILL TESTING VS.
GENERAL INTELLIGENCE TESTING

The question arises as to how to distinguish between aptitude and skill. Although there exists some overlap between the two, a test of skill normally measures what a person has already learned about a particular job, while a test of aptitude measures an individual's capacity to learn required skills. The latter predicts performance, while the former measures performance.

Aptitude testing developed out of psychologists' involvement in vocational guidance, and also in the selection process for business and industry. Most experts believe that, while general intelligence tests do measure a number of different factors, they do not distinguish among an individual's levels of ability on each of those factors.

Some general intelligence tests do segment scores for separate areas of intelligence. But specialists feel that tests which measure just one of the abilities—verbal ability, numerical ability, perceptual speed, spatial ability, reasoning ability—are more reliable predictors of job success.

It is also true that general intelligence tests measure various mental abilities, but offer no performance rating for physical abilities. Studies have shown that there is usually no relationship between the two, so a person's score in one area has no predictive value in the other. The result is the development of a variety of mental and physical tests that measure a variety of aptitudes for a variety of jobs.

COMMON BUSINESS APTITUDE TESTS

Here is a list of the kinds of aptitude tests most often used in the selection process in business and industry.

- *Mental tests* assess an individual's intellectual capacity only.

- *Intelligence tests* are still used as a screening tool in some industrial settings.

- *Tests of quick recall* typically require the applicant to look briefly at a long number—usually ten digits—and then turn the test paper over and reproduce the number on the other side.

- *Rapid learning tests* offer problems in lists of letters and arbitrary numerical equivalents. For example, the applicant is told that A = 7, B = 3, C = 4, etc. Then the person is presented with a message written in letters and required to translate it into numbers, or vice versa.

- *Tests of mechanical comprehension* at varying levels of difficulty measure the abilities required in jobs ranging from auto mechanic to engineer.

- *General mechanical knowledge tests* present, usually in picture form, problems designed to explore a person's knowledge of gears, levers, pulleys, and similar objects.

- *Comprehension of spatial relations tests* typically show a group of shapes, and then ask into which of several whole figures they will fit.

- *Tests of accurate perception* require an ability to distinguish between numbers and letters that are almost the same, or to untangle a jumbled printed pattern.

- *Number and name matching tests* present a person with pairs of many-digit numbers or long names with some of the pairs identical and others differing by one character. The applicant has to designate which pairs are the same and which are different.

- *Tests of perceptual persistence* many include a series of jumbled, crisscross lines which require the person being tested to separate each of them from the tangle.

- *Motor abilities tests* comprise a group in which hand and eye movements are tested for speed and dexterity. They include:

  — *following a path* in which a series of parallel lines broken at different random points is shown. The applicant must draw a line quickly through those openings.

  — *fine dotting tests* where the person being tested is shown a series of very small squares or cubes, and is required to quickly put one or more dots in the center of each.

  — *manual dexterity tests* which vary depending on whether fine or gross movements are being tested. Some tests involve putting very small pegs into holes, or assembling them into a small figure. Others involve handling blocks in a sequential order, or packing them into a container.

15

MEASURES
OF INTEREST

An individual's success in a job generally results from two factors—aptitude and interest. However well equipped a person may be to perform well in a specific area of responsibility, if he or she has no interest in it, the chances for failure are high.

A highly skilled professional counselor can use a lengthy interview to elicit enough information from an applicant to form an intelligent opinion of whether that individual would be happy/satisfied in a particular occupation. But not many businesses have such skilled professional help.

The interest tests that are available today can produce the same information in a relatively short time. That data can then be used as a further guidepost in the search for the best person for your company's job.

"INVENTORIES" TO MEASURE INTEREST

The devices that have been developed to measure occupational interests are generally referred to as inventories rather than tests, since the results are not designed to distinguish between high and low scores. The main purpose of such tests is to predict the kind of job the applicant is most likely to enjoy—and therefore remain at with appropriate levels of enthusiasm.

All the inventories are based on widely substantiated research which shows that people successfully engaged in specific occupations have common interests that clearly separate them from people pursuing other occupational careers. These distinctive interests include areas related to performing their jobs, as well as what those individuals like and dislike in terms of hobbies, sports, social relations and activities, plays and books, and so forth.

Scoring a Well-known Test

The best-known and probably most widely used of these measures is the Strong Campbell Interest Inventory, a revision of the pioneering Strong Vocational Interest Blank. This particular test has seven parts.

In the first five, the individual responding indicates whether he or she *likes*, *dislikes*, or is *indifferent* to the following:

1. particular occupations (131 listed);

2. school subjects (36 listed);

3. personal activities (51 listed, including taping a sprained ankle, cooking, starting a conversation with a stranger);

4. amusements (39 listed, including golf, nightclubs, preparing dinner for guests);

5. and people of various types (24 listed, including highway construction workers, babies, athletic people).

Part 6 offers 30 pairs of activities (airline pilot vs. airline ticket agent; taking a chance vs. playing it safe; teacher vs. salesperson) from which the subject chooses the one preferred.

Part 7 consists of 14 statements describing "characteristics," such as wins friends easily, puts drive into an organization. The subject responds *yes, no or ?* based on whether or not the statement accurately describes him or her.

The scoring is done on the basis of comparison with the responses of people in a specific occupation. If an individual's responses resemble those given by physicians, for example, the inference is that his or her interests are much the same as those of physicians. Experts developed the various criterion scales for scoring the tests by comparing the responses of people in a certain occupation with those of a group in the general population, thus uncovering those items where the differences in preference were clear. The inventory is scored for 162 occupational groups, including physician, banker, architect, life insurance salesperson, craftsman, chemist, and personnel manager. It can be used for both men and women.

Most follow-up studies have shown a high stability of interests over many years. A majority of people taking the tests actually enters the preferred occupations indicated by their scores, remain in them, find satisfaction in them, and achieve financial success in their jobs. A 1979 study showed a predictive validity for males of 59.3 percent and for females of 42.5 percent.

Variations in Another Widely Used Test

The Kuder Preference Record–Vocational test is another frequently used measure of vocational preference. It differs from the Strong Campbell test in three ways. First, all items deal with activities only. Second, all items are arranged in groups of three. Third, scores are given for ten general areas of interest, rather than in terms of specific occupations. The ten scales identify interests in mechanical, outdoor, computational, scientific, persuasive, artistic, literary, musical, social, science, and clerical activities. Specific related occupations are then listed under each of these headings.

Another form of testing is the Kuder Preference Record—Personal. While the Vocational test identifies an individual's preference in occupational areas, the Personal test helps determine the kind of situation in which the person prefers to work. It explores such questions as:

- How much a person likes to take part in group activities
- What role a person prefers in a group
- How interested a person is in exploring new situations
- Whether a person likes to be self-assertive
- Whether a person prefers working with ideas or with things.

Every occupation or profession requires certain social relationships, and the scores on the Personal test indicate the kind of relationships that are preferred by the individual being tested. While a particular score on the Vocational test may be applicable to several occupations, each of those occupations can be characterized by different types of personal relationships. When you develop the individual's score on both the Vocational and the Personal, therefore, you have a clearer picture of those occupations that fit both scores.

The five scales in the Kuder Preference Record—Personal are:

- Preference for being active in groups
- Preference for familiar and stable situations
- Preference for working with ideas
- Preference for avoiding conflict
- Preference for influencing others.

PITFALLS TO AVOID

One problem with interest inventories of any kind is that intelligent applicants can sometimes tailor their answers to what they think the immediate job requires. Although new editions of these measures have built-in safeguards designed to show whether a subject is faking, they are not foolproof. But you can minimize the tendency toward misleading by providing a nonthreatening environment where applicants are put at ease. You should even point out to them that less-than-candid answers are not really in their own interests.

Your company can also establish its own standards of validity for an interest inventory by administering it to current employees. It is likely that the scores will clearly differentiate among top, average, and poor performers. Once you establish such scoring standards, the possibilities of people outwitting the interest measure diminish. In fact, any individual determined to "beat" the test will usually score so high that the scores of the firm's proven top performers look low; it's a warning sign that you should look for.

As with all the measures discussed in Part II, you should not use interest inventories alone as the single determinant of whether or not to hire an individual. They should be viewed as part of the entire selection process and used in conjunction with aptitude tests, since the two factors—aptitude and interest—are mutually dependent.

16

MEASURES OF PERSONALITY OR TEMPERAMENT

"He was very good at the job, but he had a personality problem with his boss."

"The two of them just can't work on that project together—their personalities clash."

The majority of managers have heard just such statements, lamenting the loss of a good employee or the ineffectiveness of a person who should be a top performer. The reference is to some aspect of how a person approaches a job, whether it's called personality, temperament, character, nature, or attitude.

DEFINING TEMPERAMENT

A practical definition of temperament used by psychologists is "a person's behavioral tendency." Some people behave in passive ways, others in domineering fashion; some people are argumentative, others are judicious; some flexible, others rigid; one individual is sensitive, another imperturbable.

A person's temperament is basically a general way of acting over a period of time, not necessarily at any given moment. Each person forms certain habitual ways of acting. The individual whose behavioral tendency is to be argumentative will act in a variety of ways that express that tendency. He or she will protest firmly in a restaurant if a steak is not served the way it was ordered. And they will disagree strongly with what they consider an unwise move by their boss. All a person's many habits taken together are called a "component of temperament."

In general, a behavioral tendency causes concern to a prospective employer only if: (1) it is manifested in an extreme way; or (2) the components of temperament conflict with one another, leaving the person tense and anxious. In either case, such a person will not possess a well-integrated personality and will not be the best choice as a prospective employee.

HOW TEMPERAMENT IS MEASURED

Differences exist among industrial psychologists as to exactly which component factors of personality are important. But the experts do agree that a person's future behavior can best be predicted by past and current behavior. For that reason, most test developers utilize inventories. They ask questions designed to reveal a person's account of past behavior, as well as current attitudes, feelings, and beliefs about a variety of situations.

One well-known personality inventory is the Guilford-Zimmerman Temperament Survey. It asks three hundred questions which give positive and negative scores for ten behavioral areas:

- General Activity
- Restraint
- Ascendance
- Sociability
- Emotional Stability
- Objectivity
- Friendliness
- Thoughtfulness
- Personal Relations
- Masculinity

The principal value of this test for industry is its demonstrated ability to identify potential instigators of problems.

One of the most widely used measures of personality in business is the Personality Inventory, developed by Dr. Robert G. Bernreuter. It consists of 125 items demanding three responses—*yes, no, or ?*. It yields six scores:

- Neurotic Tendency
- Self-Sufficiency
- Introversion-Extroversion
- Dominance-Submission
- Sociability
- Confidence

Other Useful Personality Inventories

Another personality test, the Holland Vocational Preference

Inventory, uses occupational titles as its content. The individual indicates "interest" or "dislike" for 160 items. This type of test rests on the rationale that occupational preference reflects a great deal more about a person than knowledge of the requirements of the job. The Holland test measures eleven components:

- Realistic

- Intellectual

- Social

- Conventional

- Enterprising

- Artistic

- Self-Control

- Masculinity

- Status

- Infrequency

- Acquiescence

The Survey of Personal Values, a part of the Holland test, measures six critical values that influence how an individual copes with the problems and choices of everyday living. The values are practical-mindedness, achievement, variety, decisiveness, orderliness, and goal orientation. This provides information on how a person is likely to approach a job or training program. The scores reflect the relative weight an individual places on each value. The test uses three-part items in which the person must label one "most important" and one "least important." This forced-choice method makes it difficult for the individual taking the test to figure out the "desired" answer, and tends to elicit candid responses.

On-the-job Business Measurements

The Gordon Personal Profile and Inventory, a two-part test, measures eight behavioral components including ascendancy, responsibility, emotional stability, sociability, cautiousness, original thinking, personal relations, and vigor. It has been shown to predict successful on-the-job performance in a number of professional and clerical activities.

The test uses four-part questions, where the person must choose one most like himself or herself, and one least like. The questions are designed so that two parts look equally favorable, and two look equally unfavorable, making it more difficult to "fake" one's answers by trying to figure out which are "right." It is a relatively short test, which can be given in fifteen minutes.

Another well-known inventory is the Thurstone Temperament Schedule, which measures seven personality traits:

- *Active*—works and moves rapidly.

- *Vigorous*—participates in physical activity.

- *Impulsive*—carefree disposition; makes decisions quickly.

- *Dominant*—leadership ability; capable of taking initiative and responsibility.

- *Stable*—cheerful, even disposition.

- *Sociable*—enjoys company of others.

- *Reflective*—thinks meditatively; enjoys theoretical problems.

The California Psychological Inventory (CPI) is particularly extensive, offering eighteen measurements in four categories. The first is Poise, Ascendancy, and Self-Assurance (dominance, capacity for status, sociability, social presence, self-acceptance, sense of well-being).

The second category measures Socialization, Character, Responsibility, and Interpersonal Values (responsibility, socialization, self-control, tolerance, good impression, communality).

The third involves Achievement, Potential, and Intellectual Efficiency (achievement via conformance, achievement via independence, intellectual efficiency). And the fourth measures Intellectual and Interest Modes (psychological-mindedness, flexibility, femininity).

The CPI scales are based on the actual test responses of people known to exhibit the kinds of effective behavior it is measuring. It contains three internal checks on the validity of responses to guard against faking and is most useful in situations where an employer wants to identify achievement-oriented people.

The Myers-Briggs Type Indicator measures personality dispositions and interests, and is based on the theories of the world-renowned psychologist Karl Jung. It provides scores on four scales: Introversion-Extroversion; Sensing-Intuition; Thinking-Feeling; Judging-Perceptive. Its principal value in business is in management-development programs and career guidance for managers.

UTILIZATION OF PERSONALITY TESTS

Harlan Jones, as director of staffing and development for General Telephone of the Southwest, claimed that a combination of these tests gave invaluable assistance and information to the company, as well as to the manager or potential manager.

General Telephone of the Southwest tested high-potential people recommended by its current managers. Some of those tested were already managers, others were seen as management material. The process is voluntary and confidential. The results are reported only to the individuals taking the test, and they are not required to discuss the results with anyone or to take any action. But about 80 percent of them do discuss their results with their superiors.

According to Jones, the employees who take the tests learn how effective they are—or are likely to be—in situations in which they supervise others. They also learn their shortcomings. As a result of the feedback, some people drop out of the management race; others decide that they're satisfied with the status quo. After discussing the results with their own managers, however, most choose to work on modifying whatever behaviors they can change to further their managerial careers.

Those people who choose not to discuss their test results are not forced to, says Jones. But such an attitude is duly noted by the reluctant employee's superiors. "It [the tests] gives us the managers we want, and has been doing so for more than thirty years," said Jones. "Plus it is a source of invaluable information for the individual in both his professional and personal life."

Career Redirection

Arnold Stillman, of Corporate Dynamics, California, career-guidance counselors, said that "Through the use of such tests, hundreds of people have been redirected into new careers which are more personally satisfying and financially rewarding."

For example, Stillman revealed that many accountants came to Corporate Dynamics because they were uncomfortable in their current occupation, and not certain why. Testing proved them to be heavily extroverted people, with a need for contact with others.

"We pointed out that their present occupation gave them contact principally with paper and numbers, rather than with other people," said Stillman. "For many, this was the first step in a happy change to other occupations such as marketing, retailing, and so forth. These tests have not only helped turn people's lives around, but have provided as much assistance to the companies these people left as to those they joined in their new careers."

Personality Tests at the Entry Level

Although the majority of firms that use personality measures in the personnel process incorporate them into their management-development programs, such inventories have value at lower levels as well. Joseph Fitzhugh, as president of Automotive Training Corporation of America, is such a user.

His enterprise trains entry-level service advisors for the service departments of automobile dealers. The job essentially involves handling customer complaints and passing the information to the repair staff.

Fitzhugh administers an inventory that classifies people by type: introvert-extrovert, thinking-feeling, and so forth. His familiarity with various service managers who recruit from his organization enables him to refer his graduates to prospective employers with whom there will be no personality clashes.

Fitzhugh said that he employed the same personality inventory when he was the West Coast training manager with Volkswagen, Porsche, and Audi of America. The measure "played a large part in reducing the annual turnover in service-shop management from 150 percent to 15–20 percent."

17

VALIDATING
YOUR TESTS

Certain tests will work well as predictors or classifiers for another company, but there is no guarantee that it will do as well for yours. As an employer, you must determine if a particular test performs the function that you intend it to for your organization. This process of learning whether or not a test works is called *validation*.

Every reputable test publisher validates its tests on some group before offering it for use. A test of mechanical aptitude may be administered to new employees of one or more companies, and the scores recorded. Over a specific period—for instance, a year or two—the progress of those who took the test is observed and recorded. At the end of that period, a comparison is made between the employees' ranking on the test and the level of mechanical skill they achieve on the job.

There are statistical guidelines which determine how closely the two sets of ranking should match and how large a testing group should be used. A test that falls within those guidelines is labeled valid.

VARIOUS TYPES OF VALIDITY

Test-makers demand various types of validity depending on the type of test and its purpose.

Face validity   Refers to whether or not the test appears, on its initial reading, to be testing what it purports to measure. The importance of face validity lies in the test-taker's reaction. A person who expects a test of mechanical knowledge and instead finds a question on who first formulated various mechanical principles, might reasonably conclude that the test is not doing what it is supposed to—and thus is "unfair." The astute employer must avoid the obviously negative emotional environment created for the test-taker in that situation.

Content validity.   Takes an important step beyond face validity. While a test may appear to be valid (face validity), in reality it may not be testing the *ability to perform* a specific kind of task.

Here's an example. Suppose you need a test of a person's knowledge and ability as a legal stenographer. A publisher produces one that consists only of the rapid dictation of material heavily laden with legal terms, along with the requirement that the material be typed quickly and accurately. That certainly seems to be valid.

But the legal stenographer you need usually deals with a variety of complex legal forms that must be filled out within strict rules. Completing those forms involves 50 percent of the prospective employee's work time. That particular test—while it has face validity—does not have sufficient content validity for your needs.

Concurrent validity.   The question must be asked about how well a test discriminates among various levels of already achieved skills and abilities.

Take a group of welders rated by their supervisors as "adequate," "good," and "excellent." Give the entire group, plus a group of newly employed apprentices, a practical welding test.

The results combine the scores into two groups. Mixed together in the lower group are the "adequate" welders and the apprentices. In the second group are the "good" and "excellent" welders. This test does not have sufficient concurrent validity; it does not differentiate finely enough for the purpose at hand.

Construct validity.   Put yourself in the position of an employer who wants to devise a paper-and-pencil test that ranks auto mechanics. You call on some "experts" and select problems for the test submitted by a group of currently employed mechanics who possess a wide range of abilities. You expect that the test scores will actually correlate with the various levels of skill possessed by the people who helped to devise it.

In actual practice, though, the scores might show no match at all with what people can actually do; that often happens in the course of developing a test. Until the problem is clarified and corrected, the test lacks construct validity.

Predictive validity.   A test needs this quality to predict future achievement. Without such validity, a test loses one of its most important business characteristics— the ability to identify those individuals among the newly hired employees who will succeed best on the job.

VALIDATING YOUR OWN TESTS

Every company that uses a test, regardless of how well validated it has been by the publisher, needs to validate it for itself. You can accomplish this in several ways, keeping in mind EEO considerations at all times.

If you are using a test for predictive purposes, administer the test to a group of incoming employees. After a period of time in keeping with the requirements of your business has elapsed, rate the employees in terms of the skills they have acquired. If the scores match, the test is valid for your purposes.

If you plan to use testing for promotion or advanced training purposes, you must have concurrent validity. Administer a test to a group of current employees who have been carefully rated. Again, compare the test scores to those ratings. A close match reinforces the validity required for the instrument to be useful.

The supervisors/managers who do the ratings that will be matched with test scores should never know ahead of time what scores have been achieved. Otherwise, it will be very difficult for them to be objective in their ratings. If they think that tests are not valuable, they may try to prove it in the ratings they issue. And if they support tests, they may try to bolster the results. Ideally, the ratings should be obtained before the tests are even administered.

You may wish to use outside objective observers to interpret the results you get. Many test publishers offer validation services for a fee.

TESTING FOR RELIABILITY

In addition to a test actually measuring what it purports to, for it to be valid it must give the same results consistently.

That quality is called reliability. For example, a mechanical-aptitude test might indeed show a close enough correlation between its scores and the new employees' subsequent achievement to have apparent predictive validity. But if it does not achieve similar levels of results with each group of new employees who take it, it would be unreliable and therefore invalid.

A test cannot be valid unless it is also reliable, but reliability alone does not confer validity. A test might consistently give the same results for similar groups without actually testing what it is supposed to be measuring.

Causes of Unreliability

A principal cause of unreliability is difficulty in the construction of the test itself. Test-makers safeguard against that problem by taking the steps discussed later in this chapter.

Another important cause of unreliability is unstandardized administration. Scores on tests can be fairly compared—not only among individuals, but from one session to another (reliability measurement)—only if the conditions under which they are administered are the same.

Take an extreme case. You test two people for a clerk/typist position. The first gets an electronic typewriter in a quiet room with no distractions. The second must move to a different area using a manual typewriter and with people racing around and talking in groups. Obviously, the two results cannot be fairly compared.

The lighting in a test room, the noise level, the number of other test-takers, the test administrator's voice, manner, and responses to questions, the time allowed for completion—all must be the same each time the test is given to an individual or a group. If they are not, the probable unreliability of scores produced cannot be attributed with any certainty to the test itself. As a manager charged with responsibility for test administration, you must be on guard to maintain standardization.

Unstandardized grading can also cause unreliability. Tests which call for judgment on what constitutes a correct answer will induce differences in interpretation when different people score the test on different occasions.

Even a single manager's criteria for judging results may vary from time to time. To avoid or at least to minimize these differences, you should encourage agreement among the various examiners to make the criteria for correct answers as precise as possible.

In most tests, an employer is likely to use questions to which only one answer is correct. Or the test-marker may receive a sheet supplied by the publisher with only correct answers shown. This makes marking a virtually automatic process. On the other hand, you can usually return measures of interest or personality—which require interpretation—to the publisher for scoring.

Another item that has an impact on test reliability is the fact that personal situations may vary considerably for an individual from one test session to another. A test-taker may be ill, tired, under a particular emotional strain, upset by a sleepless night, bothered by a bad trip to work. These and other possibilities can account for sharply differing test performances from one to time to the next.

Most businesses will be working with the scores of groups, not of individuals, in establishing procedures to insure reliability. This lessens the chance of such a problem having a major impact on a test.

Insuring Reliability

Test producers use a number of techniques to insure reliability in their products. The first method likely to be applied is *retesting*. If the same people achieve substantially the same scores in two consecutive testing sessions, reliability has been strongly evidenced. Using this technique is not, however, as simple as it sounds.

In the case of a paper-and-pencil test, you must allow enough time to elapse so that the test-takers are not likely to remember their answers from the first session. But you can't allow too much time to go by, for then those individuals may have acquired new knowledge that will raise their scores.

When you administer a "hands-on" performance measure for the second time, the possibility exists that some learning took place the first time and that it will affect the new score. Here, too, the time between tests must be carefully selected. You can see that the retesting process requires considerable professional skill and judgment.

Another method for increasing reliability involves alternate forms. This amounts to constructing—and then validating—a test designed to measure the same quality as a test already in existence. The test-maker must be sure that the two forms are really equivalent.

The tests should contain the same number of items, be written (or constructed) in the same way, and include the same type of material. The level of difficulty should be the same, as well as the breadth of knowledge required. And the tests should establish the same levels of validity.

The employer enjoys two practical values from tests available in two (or more) alternate forms. First, if you are testing several people at the same time, the opportunity for cheating is reduced. Second, the opportunity for one candidate to pass on information to the next test-taker is also minimized.

A third reliability measure depends on internal division. Some test-makers divide their tests in half, and score each half separately, as well as scoring the whole. They don't necessarily divide the first half versus the second half. Fatigue or the pressure of time can affect the results on the second half negatively. Conversely, the first-half practice might raise people's scores on the second half.

To avoid these difficulties, most test-makers utilizing this method use an odd-even split of questions. This kind of division also deals adequately with a test in which the items grow progressively more difficult from beginning to end.

For the business manager, the two simplest and most practical ways to establish the reliability of a particular test are: (1) after its validity has been established in a particular group, administer it to the same group later and compare the scores. If they are essentially the same, it is reliable for the purposes of that organization. Or, (2) go through the whole validation process with a second group. If results are comparable, reliability is established.

After you have followed these processes to completion, your company will then own a uniquely valuable personnel selection tool. In general, validity and reliability need to be established only once. After that, administering the test can save effort, time and money.

ADMINISTERING
YOUR TESTS

"Despite my years of experience," said one executive secretary, "twice I've had to start my job search from the beginning when I relocated to another part of the country. I shudder when I remember taking tests with broken typewriter stands that shook and wobbled, poor lighting, worn out typewriters and adding machines, chairs too low, or tables too high. During one speed test the copy vibrated off the typing table, and the calculator added an extra digit to every number I added."

The "tests" that this secretary took were not only unfair to her, but to her prospective employers as well. What they wanted tested—the applicant's ability to work under current company conditions—was not being tested at all.

OFFERING PROPER
PHYSICAL CONDITIONS

Administering tests involves two critical conditions—giving applicants the opportunity to show themselves at their best, with the *same* opportunity afforded to every candidate.

Here are some prime considerations:

- Make sure the equipment or test papers are available and in proper order.

- Keep the testing area itself free from noise, and off-limits to anyone not directly involved in giving or taking the test.

- Watch for potential physical hazards such as tweezers that have lost their tension in a manual dexterity test, or improperly sharpened pencils ready for a written test.

- Be aware of physical amenities such as adequate lighting, comfortable temperature, sufficient space, and so forth.

- Give test-takers in a pencil-and-paper test a desk or writing table with ample room. Studies have shown that people taking tests in chairs with writing arms do less well than those given a desk.

ATTRIBUTES OF
THE EXAMINER

The person administering the test is a critical influence on the testing process. He or she must conscientiously enforce recommendations and standards regarding tools, equipment, and environment—and must do it the same way every time. A quiet room for one applicant and a noisy room for another means that, in reality, they did not take the same test. The examiner assumes a position of utmost importance for the candidate's performance in five areas.

INSTRUCTIONS AND
ANSWERING QUESTIONS

Relatively simple test situations permit oral instructions. Generally, instructions should be read aloud to the examinees, so that every individual, every time, hears exactly the same ones. Most published tests come with instructions to be read by the examiner.

"I asked the examiner a question about the sample question on mechanics," said one test-taker. "He answered me so extensively that I was able to answer three questions on the test itself which I wouldn't otherwise have attempted. I ought to give him half my score." That comment was made about an examiner who was trying to relax the candidate, but went too far.

To avoid that pitfall, you should decide in advance the precise wording of answers to questions most frequently asked by people taking the test. Repeat them verbatim every single time. When questions arise for which no answers have been prepared, answer them briefly. Then add them to the group for which there are prepared answers.

THE QUESTION OF TIMING

Timing can influence test results in two ways. First, out of misdirected sympathy, an examiner may allow an individual, or even a group, more than the alloted amount of time. Every extra second, however, represents a change in the standardized conditions for the test. Such an act compromises both its validity and reliability. The scores achieved become worthless measures to use in judging the candidates who've been given the extra time. Also, an examiner who does it once is likely to do it again. But every time he or she *does not* do it, or gives more or less extra time, the results are further contaminated.

Another potential abuse of timing is using a stopwatch or bell in such a way that it creates anxiety in the people taking the test. Ringing a bell or clicking a stopwatch and shouting "Go" from behind the candidates' backs, can set up a tension reaction that depresses potential scores. Your "start" and "stop" instructions should be given from in front of the applicant or applicants in clear, well-modulated tones.

TEST-INDUCED ANXIETY

Even people who regularly take tests can become anxious when faced with an important one. A potential employee who hasn't faced such circumstances recently is likely to be even more nervous.

Two reactions may occur. First, people may feel that the test is a threat to their status or prestige. This is particularly true in a timed test, which is constructed so no one can possibly finish it. For that kind of test, include in the instructions the admonition that "nobody is expected to finish this test, so don't get upset when you realize that you're not going to." Without that knowledge, many test-takers will grow increasingly tense as time passes and the questions become more difficult. They simply will not perform up to their potential.

Another effect of test anxiety is a defensive posture. To relieve the tension they are feeling, some people assume a "who cares?" attitude and simply do not try their best. In such cases the test does not test what it is designed to test.

The examiner can combat this problem by calmly point-ing out that if the job is worth applying for, the test is worth the applicants' best efforts. At the same time the test ad-ministrator, while selling the value of doing one's best, must be careful to avoid making the test sound like the most important event that ever occurred.

THE SELF-FULFILLING PROPHECY

Study after study, in both academic and work environments, has demonstrated conclusively the existence of the self-fulfilling prophecy. That occurs when the person adminis-tering a test *expects* a high, mediocre, or poor performance. The person taking the test is subtly—but powerfully—in-fluenced to respond at just that level.

A group of teachers, for example, was told by school principals that certain new children had previously been high achievers, and others low achievers. The performance of the children during the following period was remarkably close to those reports. But the information that had been given to the teachers was inaccurate. It had been imparted only for the purposes of the study.

The teachers expected certain levels of achievement from the children. They unintentionally and unwittingly imparted those expectations to the children. And the children, in turn, also without realizing it, were strongly influenced by their teachers' expectations and performed accordingly. Similar results have occurred in factories when supervisors were told—also incorrectly—that new employees had scored high, medium or low, on aptitude tests.

In the testing situation, therefore, examiners must de-velop and project a warm, natural manner, without giving any indication as to the level of difficulty the candidates are likely to find in dealing with the test.

DANGER IN REPORTING SCORES

Another problem area can arise because the examiner can influence the candidates' performance even after they are actually hired. By telling their new supervisors, for instance, that one new employee scored high, another in the middle, and a third toward the low end of the scale, the examiner is almost surely planting preconceived notions in the supervisors' minds.

Even more dangerous is telling the supervisor the person's actual score. Many times that number is misconstrued in the supervisor's mind as an intelligence quotient (IQ), a term that has acquired an undeserved mystique. This happens even when the test has nothing at all to do with measuring intelligence.

It is better—if you are the administrator—to tell the supervisor that the general rule of your organization is that anyone who has successfully completed the entire recruitment process, including testing, is deemed likely to succeed. Keeping all test results confidential hurts no one. It is more likely to help both the individual and the organization.

You should treat rejected candidates in a similar manner. Rather than tell them that their test results were poor, tell them that, based on the total picture presented by their interviews, experience, education, test scores, etc., you feel that the particular job opening and their particular talents did not mesh well. (A sample rejection letter appears in Chapter 29.)

This is not just kinder—it is true. For no firm that rejects a candidate, including yours, can be *certain* that it made a perfect decision. Although the history of testing indicates that most rejected candidates who don't meet the company's own criteria would fail on the job, and most accepted candidates will make it, no one positively knows the final outcome.

TRAINING THE TEST ADMINISTRATOR

Your testing program is no better than the person who administers it. That individual—even if it's you—must be totally prepared to handle all the responsibilities discussed.

Every test from a publisher comes with a manual. It not only gives details on how the test was developed, and the kinds of jobs for which it has been validated, but also contains specific instructions for the examiner. He or she must study such manuals diligently, and follow exactly the directions for administration of the test.

Many managers experienced in this field recommend that the *examiner* take the test by enlisting the aid of another staff person. Such a practice session will reveal potential problems in the testing situation which can be solved before any employees or candidates are tested.

IMPLEMENTING SECURITY MEASURES

A test is no test at all if the candidates know even one of the questions in advance. But some organizations take minimal or no security measures. Test materials should be kept under lock and key, with possession of the key rigidly controlled. Only the examiner, and perhaps one other responsible person, should have access to them—whether it is a paper-and-pencil test or a hands-on piece of equipment.

When you use test papers more than once, number them. Make sure they are all accounted for at the end of every session, before the people taking the test leave the room. Also scrutinize the tests afterward for any notations which could give clues to future examinees. Any such paper should simply be discarded by shredding or burning.

If you suspect that security has been compromised, abandon the test and substitute another form of it. If you can't obtain another form, use a totally different test. That might mean going through the entire validation process again. This emphasizes the critical importance of enforcing security measures in the first place.

CHOOSING THE TARGET JOBS

Your company should certainly not begin a new testing program by including all, or even most, of its jobs in the process. A thorough analysis by the appropriate management people should narrow the target to one job or, at the most, two. It should be a problem job that has been consistently difficult to fill correctly.

If training doesn't seem to work, people quit frequently, productivity is low, and supervisors haven't been able to improve the situation—that job needs help. In such a situation, you will quickly see whether or not adding testing to the selection process is instrumental in solving the problem.

Don't be intimidated by the seemingly formidable process of choosing the job to be the first target, selecting the test, setting up an administrative procedure, selecting and training the examiner, and validating the results. But be aware that: (1) most managers have difficulty finding time for additional duties; and (2) such a new project will seem foreign to most managers' responsibilities and experiences.

One way you can ease this process is to employ an industrial psychologist to help get the program started. Most states have an association of professional psychologists that can refer you to experts in your area. Generally you'll only need a relatively short training period to get started. Some small companies, however, utilize industrial psychologists to administer their entire testing programs, either on a per-job basis, or for an annual retainer.

PERFORMANCE APPRAISAL: ADJUNCT TO TESTING

Your organization uses tests for one major purpose: to help select those people who will do the best job. A performance-appraisal system measures the ensuing results, not what employees are *likely to do*, but what they *have done*. At the same time, you can evaluate your tests' effectiveness by what performance appraisals reveal about the people who were selected.

HOW PERFORMANCE APPRAISAL FITS IN

Additionally, performance appraisals help provide solutions to such management problems as excessive turnover, scarcity of skilled employees, the readiness of entry-level employees for promotion, or the effectiveness of line managers.

Employees frequently wonder just how they are rated by their supervisors, whether they are slated for advancement, raises, or training. When you integrate performance appraisals into your organization's pattern, people almost always will perform more effectively.

The larger your organization, the more difficult it is to maintain effective control of human resources and to measure how well those resources are being utilized. Performance appraisal plays an important role in both measurement and control in several areas.

DEVELOPMENT OF TRAINING PROGRAMS

Without the benefit of an organized performance-appraisal system, management might complain: "We simply don't have enough skilled machinists (or welders or stenographers)." The progressive company, on the other hand, will be able to say: "One year from now, our own training programs will be providing 80 percent of the welders we need, and in two years we will be able to train all our welders in-house."

In the second situation, an organized performance-appraisal system tells management just how many apprentice welders it has, as well as the objectives—such as time frame—for their development. Also, the same program will tell the organization's manpower planners just how many entry-level factory workers have been assessed as being ready for the welder-apprentice program.

The training department can then forecast how many people will receive skills-improvement training, and how many of that group will successfully complete the program. Furthermore, experience will tell the planning group just how many of the successful trainees will remain with the company.

All these results enhance the company's ability to forecast how its personnel needs will be filled. Basic to all the analyzing and forecasting is an appropriate appraisal system. And the firm that can use such a system in the area of welders, can also do the same with its stenographers, its long-haul truck drivers, its management trainees, and so forth.

Another important advantage accrues to a firm having command of this kind of information. Individual department and group managers spend less valuable time wondering how they are going to fill their quotas, and more time concentrating on other productive duties.

SETTING COMPANY GOALS

Most firms develop not only specific long-term goals—dollar and volume, market penetration, collection, etc.—but also interim one-year goals as part of their overall planning process. Specific goal-setting for each individual is an integral part of every performance-appraisal system, so that system makes an important contribution to the company's total goal-setting efforts.

Successive layers of management are appraised and their goals set. Managers repeat the process at each level below, developing specific contributions to the overall goal for each. Eventually top management obtains a clear picture of how it is moving toward its corporate goals.

TRACKING GOOD EMPLOYEES

Some firms require managers at all levels to maintain an ongoing detailed record on the potential promotability of each of their subordinates. Company executives monitor these surveys at all times. Managers report on subordinates' potential in such areas as:

- outstanding ability;
- necessary improvement;
- potential for leadership;
- availability for transfer to other divisions or other geographic locations;
- relationships with their subordinates, peers and supervisors;
- upper management potential;
- overall evaluation;
- and specific educational/training/other plans for enhancing that potential.

A company with such an inventory of its people will never lack for managers at any level.

A performance-appraisal system must exist so a company can not only maintain a management inventory, but can answer such questions as:

—Do we have the group of managers we will need to run the new plant we're opening next year?

—If they are not all available now, how many are we short, in what areas, and will an immediate training program fill the gaps?

—Are we grooming enough financial personnel, manufacturing directors, marketing people?

—Can the potential management shortages in one of our plants be filled by people available in another?

—Who are the people most likely to be leading this company ten years from now?

Many high-level executives also measure their managers' performances by the performance of their subordinates. If one manager's subordinates are performing considerably above or below the level of their peers in other groups, top management is alerted.

In any organization where appraisals are used this way, the potential for self-serving performance appraisals is apparent. To counteract this, companies develop appraisal systems in which each individual is appraised not only by a manager, but by the manager's manager as well. Some firms even utilize a committee chosen from an individual's subordinates and peers, and from colleagues of the manager.

Carrying this system one step further, a company can base its raises, promotions, educational opportunities, and other benefits to its employees on an appraisal system that measures everyone by the same criteria.

ADVANTAGES TO EMPLOYEES FROM PERFORMANCE APPRAISALS

In general, a performance-appraisal system tells employees what is expected of them,, how well they are fulfilling those expectations, and what they and the company can do to correct or enhance their performances.

In particular, feedback is necessary for employees to know what they need to do to improve their performances.

Performance appraisals tell employees at all levels where they stand currently, what their supervisors think of their performances, and the reasons for the rewards they, or their colleagues, have gained. Most people, given the opportunity and incentive, want to improve what they do. Performance appraisals tell them how.

Performance appraisals help make standards clear. An employee being rated on specific criteria knows precisely what is expected. It may be to produce a certain number of subassemblies per hour; to evaluate and rate so many policy applications; to answer specific quotas of customer complaints; to keep maintenance costs within certain monetary limits; or to reduce employee turnover by a certain percentage. Whatever the standard, the employee understands what goals are to be attained.

A performance-appraisal session always includes a discussion of future performance goals and specific ways in which those goals can be achieved.

This kind of counseling can turn a frustrating job into a challenging task, a boring assignment into a fulfilling adventure.

CONDUCTING A
PERFORMANCE APPRAISAL

If you're conducting the appraisal session with a subordinate, set up the meeting in a quiet office. Discuss how the employee has performed over the last year or six months on the basis of a list of specific criteria. Make it a conversation and dialogue, not a set of pronouncements. Try to reach agreement on the past period's results.

Next you should discuss goals for the coming year, reaching agreement and recording them. Allow time to consider how those goals can be attained, problems that may develop, and how they can best be solved. Note any special training, education, or other assistance that will be required.

Then talk about the person's prospects, needs, hopes for the future, and how they may ultimately be realized. A salary review may or may not be part of the appraisal. That differs from company to company. Most experts agree that that review should entail a separate meeting.

Prior to Performance Appraisal

Before a job performance can be appraised, the job itself must be defined and performance standards established (see Part I). Both job definitions and performance standards should be objective, observable, and capable of being documented, as well as job-related, not person-related.

The Office of Personnel Management of the U.S. government has developed a performance-appraisal system based on those criteria and divided into three basic components.

The first is functional activity. This describes the job a person does, but not the reason why. An individual may spend most of the time, for example, reading and writing reports, instructing subordinates, attending meetings, and writing letters. The job description specifies these as functional activities.

The second component is job elements. These are the purposes of the job, the results you want achieved. Take, for example, a person who supervises die cutters in a machine shop. That is *what* is done, the functional activity. *Why* it's done is to produce machined parts. That is the job element.

Most jobs have more than one required functional activity. A job element, that is, a result to be achieved, must be established for each.

The third component is performance standards. These are the yardsticks for measuring the attainment of the required job elements. For example, one job element for a supervisor of die cutters is to keep down the rejection rates for machined parts. You might express the performance standard for that job element as follows: Performance is satisfactory when the monthly rejection rate is 5 percent or less, as shown in the quarterly reports over a one-year period. Usually these standards are set by an agreement between the supervisor and subordinate after analyzing the job together.

TWO PRIME SOURCES
OF TESTING INFORMATION

In order to give you an idea of what's actually available on the employee testing scene today, this chapter reviews information provided by two highly respected companies operating in the testing field.

There are many other firms engaged in all aspects of testing. One of your major goals is to find the one (or more) that can do the most for your firm.

You should comb the field and find the source that best fits in with your immediate and future needs regarding testing. Many of the companies you'll look at will have characteristics similar to the two described below. By filing this information away in your personal "intelligence bank," you'll be one step ahead of the game in your search.

TEST COLLECTIONS

The Test Collection is one of the world's largest resource libraries for tests and other measurement devices. It currently comprises over eleven thousand instruments in a variety of forms. In addition to files on tests, it has listings of American and foreign publishers, test reviews, and reference materials on measurement and evaluation.

If you have a specific testing area in mind, and you'd like to know what tests are available, the Test Collection's bibliographies are easily worth their three-dollar fee.

You can see samples of what you get in Appendix A. Basically, they have the test name, publisher, description, target population and other pertinent data. To get the specific tests, write directly to the publisher or distributor. Appendix B has a list of major American publishers.

The Test Collection also had two updating services. It publishes *News on Tests* that comes out ten times per year. Each newsletter contains announcements from publishers on recent tests, as well as citations of test reviews and new reference materials for those involved in testing.

The Test Collection is also now a publicly scarchablc data base through Bibliographic Retrieval Services. It contains:

- bibliographic records of tests with descriptions and availability information;

- five thousand test records describing assessment tools used in evaluating testing;

- information on commercially available tests and non-commercial research instruments; and

- quarterly updates describing newly acquired instruments.

Among the general areas covered by Test Collection's bibliographies are:

—Achievement

—Aptitude

—Attitudes and Interests

—Personality

—Sensory-Motor

—Vocational/Occupational

SCIENCE RESEARCH ASSOCIATES, INC.

Once you settle on a specific test, you go straight to the publisher for further information. SRA is one of the largest in the United States, with headquarters at 155 North Wacker Drive, Chicago, Illinois, 60606. It also operates in Canada, England and Australia.

SRA publishes a wide range of business tests for hiring and evaluating employees, and also has a Test Validity Analysis Service and an Attitude Survey System.

Many of the major publishers produce glossy catalogues that detail their services and give examples of the tests they publish. SRA is no exception. Its 45-page *Test Catalogue for Business* covers all the tests it makes available and shows samples of many. Among the reproductions are tests for:

• Adaptability

• Clerical Aptitudes

• Computer Operator and Programmer Aptitude Battery

• Flannagan Aptitude Classification Tests

- Leadership Opinion Questionnaire
- Personal Audit
- Sales Attitude Check List
- Survey of Interpersonal Values
- Thurstone Temperament Schedule
- Typing Skills

PART III

THE INTERVIEWING PROCESS

INTRODUCTION

The hiring interview is the most crucial step in the selection process. No application, résumé, recommendation, or test has the impact of a personal meeting with an applicant. And the decision you make based on the interview can affect your company—and your career—for years to come.

Selecting the right applicant can strengthen your organization and your position and help them grow. Conversely, hiring the wrong person can be costly in time, money, and morale.

This section of the book will help ensure that you achieve the former, not the latter. It will make you a better overall interviewer with general helpful hints that can be used in many phases of your interpersonal communications.

Specifically, it will show you: how to structure meetings as well as the techniques to use to get applicants to talk freely; how to obtain information about every essential aspect of the applicant's background and probe each area for more detailed information; how to learn about the applicant's strengths and weaknesses, ambitions, and behavior patterns without cutting off the flow of information by putting the applicant on the defensive.

You'll find some updated traditional checklists and summary sheets to adapt to your own specific requirements. And you'll learn about some of the latest devices on the selection scene, like graphoanalysis.

The first chapter in this section deals with the question—and questions—of EEO. In today's interviewing atmosphere, a clear grasp of EEO ramifications has assumed paramount importance.

You'll find a host of important guidelines and suggestions in the following pages. But you should always look to the experts—legal counsel, government officials—for the specifics.

INTERVIEWING
AND EEO—WHAT YOU CAN
AND CAN'T ASK

Here are some general suggestions for the various phases of your employee interview selection process as regards EEO considerations. They are not guidelines or strictures—merely advice.

As with all EEO information, these do's and don'ts are not cast in concrete. They should be used as background to help shape your overall management style in the hiring process. In fact, some of these areas should be factored into your style no matter whom you're selecting, minority or otherwise.

You may also want to make copies to pass out to supervisory personnel under your jurisdiction, colleagues or even higher-level executives.

• Use common sense in all questioning. But also prepare with specific questions so that you don't inadvertently hit any of these touchy subjects:

(a)   Any questions not job-related;

(b)   Asking a single female about her plans for marriage;

(c)   Asking a female if she has someone to care for her children while she works, or what her plans are for having children;

(d)   Asking questions of minority applicants or females that you would not ask of nonminorities or males;

(e)   If the job involves travel, working long hours, or potential transfer, asking about attitudes of females alone;

(f)   Asking an older worker how many more years he or she plans to work.

• When you're having trouble establishing rapport with minority group members or females, relax your interview controls a little. Letting the individual ramble some can create a much better atmosphere for information exchange and add to your insight into the character of the person.

• Do not overdo rapport-setting techniques with anyone, especially members of minorities or women.

• Be careful about the warm-up period before beginning the interview itself. Interviewers have been known to make comments they later regretted regarding personal preferences.

• Be aware of your facial expressions. If yours reflect a negative reaction, they could lead to charges of discrimination. In these cases, applicants may charge that you were biased—that they "never had a chance."

- Informal conversation at the end of the interview can also create problems. As soon as you have completed the interview, thank the applicant, say you will get back to him or her, and stand up as an indication that the discussion has been concluded.

- Be especially aware of your "interruption technique" in dealing with minorities and females. Perception is the key here. They may interpret strict control and interruptions as a reflection of your attitudes toward their race, sex or handicap.

- Work histories should be carefully studied beforehand in the case of members of a group who may have suffered from previous job discrimination. In these cases, you should be more aware of potential than achievement.

- In order to probe behind a relatively weak minority job history, check out the initiative involved in obtaining previous jobs, untitled responsibilities, work hours and physical demands, and responsibility progress from job to job.

- The discussion of strengths and weaknesses with minorities and females is necessarily colored by their previous brushes with discrimination. You'll have to probe very delicately here to gain a true perspective on what is personal and what is outside the individual's control.

- Judge past responsibilities of such applicants in light of the situations in which they were involved. Don't penalize them if they don't have certain experiences because they weren't given a chance to develop their abilities.

At the same time, don't assume a capability for responsibility that might not be there. Check out the chapter in this book on how to read between the lines of résumés.

- Suspend your usual initial negative reaction to a career "job-hopper." Find out if the person was a difficult employee, or merely trying to continuously better him- or herself. They may have been operating in a different economic scenario than you're used to.

- Check on your educational standards for specific jobs. Compare those standards to what current workers have attained. If they're not comparable, you've got a problem. Artificially established standards are considered unfair and may screen out a disproportionate number of minorities and/or women.

- Strict grade requirements can mislead and also serve as an artificial barrier to candidates whose schooling was impacted by outside factors. Having to help support a family, extracurricular activities, and academic standards and atmosphere at schools attended all contribute to the level of marks attained.

- Sometimes an "informal" education can be as valuable to your company as a formal one for a new employee. For example, many physically handicapped people have been denied access to classes because of architectural factors. They may have compensated with home study or correspondence courses. Find out.

- Never indicate to members of a group such as minorities, females, or the handicapped that they are being hired because the company has an EEO program.

SENSITIVE EEO AREAS
IN INTERVIEWING

Check specifics with your legal counsel or the appropriate government agency if you have any questions on what you can and cannot cover.

But as you create your own unique interviewing style, it is advisable to understand some general parameters and incorporate them into your techniques.

Although some states have issued stricter interpretations of the laws, the federal authorities and most states permit an application form to ask age and sex of an applicant. However, they do prohibit using this information for discriminatory purposes. (See Chapter 8 for more on applications.)

Irrespective of the prohibitions that apply to you, it is inadvisable to discuss age with an applicant because it may give the applicant reason to complain that he or she was discriminated against.

Concerning asking applicants about pertinent dates, you may ask the date the applicant graduated from high school or college and the dates of employment in each job held. But again, only if such a discussion of dates is job-related.

A very touchy area for female interviewing revolves around children. No matter how much you may want to assure your company of the applicant's dependability, you can't ask a woman:

- if she has small children at home and what arrangements have been made to take care of them;

- if she is currently pregnant or is planning to have a family;

- (in all cases) about marital status and the number of children.

You can ask "Can you come to work consistently?" And "Can you work overtime on short notice?" But you must ask them of both men and women. And you should explain what you mean by "consistently" and "short notice."

OTHER SENSITIVE AREAS

Some interviewers cross over the legal line in trying to ascertain attitudes toward travel by saying to a woman "How would your husband feel about your traveling and being away from home several nights each week?" Instead, explain the amount of travel involved and suggest the applicant—male and female—discuss it with his or her family.

Another female area you have to beware of is pregnancy. You can't ask if a female is pregnant or plans to have children. And even if they look pregnant, you can't refuse them employment for that reason alone. You can refuse only if the type of work will endanger the woman.

The courts have ruled you can't inquire into arrest records because there is a disproportionate share of minorities being arrested. Also, an arrest doesn't mean conviction or even bad character on the part of the applicant. You can't even inquire about convictions unless it relates directly to the job. That means if the job could present the possibility of stealing money or merchandise, you can ask "Have you ever been convicted of a crime relating to theft, embezzlement or similar crimes?"

You may indicate to the applicant that they have to work Saturday and Sunday if all other employees do. This might affect their religious practices. You can't automatically refuse to hire if an applicant claims to not be able to work one of those days—unless you can show later on in the event of a complaint that it would cause the company undue hardship.

The physical area is also sensitive. Again, the job-related requirements are paramount. You can't just ask "How is your health?" or read a list of ailments and ask "Have you ever had any of these?"

What you *can* do is to explain the job's physical requirements and ask "Is there any reason why you cannot do this job satisfactorily?"

SOME FINAL THOUGHTS ON EEO AND INTERVIEWING

A good rule to follow when interviewing an applicant is to limit questions to those which are directly pertinent and important to the successful performance of the job. This does not limit you to specifics such as "How fast do you type?" or "How many units of merchandise did you sell?" You can ask questions on intangibles such as motivation, creativity, perseverance and other personal factors. You should word them so it is clear that the questions clearly relate to the job.

The safest course for interviewers to take is to keep up with the constant changes in interpretation of the Equal Employment Opportunity laws. Subscribe to one of the services that provides this information. Read the various personnel publications which usually carry this type of information.

QUESTIONS YOU MAY HAVE
ON EEO QUESTIONING

To be a better employment interviewer and to do your job properly, you must be thoroughly familiar with the various state and federal laws concerning EEO.

Always keep in mind that the job-relatedness of the questions and whether the questions you ask the applicants have a different effect on minorities, are key factors in determining the legitimacy of the question.

Here are some common general questions and their answers which you should know. If you have a specific question, you should ask your attorney or the appropriate government agency.

1. On an application form or in an interview, can I ask the name of the next of kin?
   You can't even ask whom to notify in case of an emergency, since this may show national origin if the name is different than the applicant's.

2. What about asking what foreign languages they speak?
   You can ask that, but not how they learned them.

3. Can I advertise and specify: "Recent college graduate preferred"?
   No, because it implies age discrimination in favor of youth.

4. Can I ask the applicant if he or she owns a car?
   Only if the car is needed for the job itself.

5. Can I ask about immigration visas?
   Yes, because aliens working in this country need a green card (permanent immigration visa).

6. How about arrests and convictions?

If it has a direct bearing on the job (money handling, security), you can ask if the applicant has any felony convictions. Otherwise no. The EEO Commission has ruled that it is unlawful to refuse to hire a minority applicant because of a conviction unless the circumstances make the employment "manifestly inconsistent with the safe and efficient operation of the job."

7. Can I refuse to employ a pregnant woman?

Only if the work may endanger her health.

8. Can I use a publisher's vouchsafe that a test is nondiscriminatory?

No. It must be validated against your company's experience.

9. Can I ask a woman applicant if she has small children at home?

What makes it discriminatory to do that is that the question is not normally asked of men. Don't ask.

10. Can I specify an age preference if the job requires a lot of travel?

No, because ability to handle travel doesn't correlate to age. You also can't ask for a male applicant if a lot of travel is involved.

11. Can I have a job that calls for someone "at least twenty-one"?

This is not an acceptable reason for age discrimination.

12. How about if I need an attractive woman as my receptionist to greet visitors?

No go.

GETTING READY
TO INTERVIEW

The selection procedure can be divided into four steps:

1. Submission of an application
2. Screening interview
3. Selection interview
4. Job-offer interview.

The application elicits the basic information that you as the hiring manager need to determine whom to consider seriously, whom to see only as a courtesy and those persons not to see at all.

The screening interview weeds out applicants who do not meet basic requirements. It is usually brief—fifteen minutes are enough. The interview questions determine the applicant's knowledge of key job factors. For example, if the job requires familiarity with cost accounting, you ask the applicants to describe their responsibilities for cost accounting in previous jobs. If the responses indicate insufficient knowledge, you can just end the meeting. If there are only a few candidates, the screening interview can be combined with the selection interview.

The selection interview is the most important step in the hiring process. In a meeting that should take an hour or more, you should get the vital information on which to base your final hiring decision. Some managers ask a colleague to conduct an interview before making their final choice. You yourself may have asked, or been asked, to perform this service in the past.

You can use this "sharing" process in several ways. The most obvious advantage is that it will strengthen your own selection abilities by adding the extra ingredients of objectivity and different perspective.

You'll also strength your ties with colleagues and peers by offering—as well as soliciting—interview aid. The more you make yourself available, the more esteem you'll generate in other managers.

And by honing your selection skills with this book, and getting the word out through managerial interaction, you'll draw the attention of top-level management as a skilled interviewer working in the best interests of the company.

For the head of a small business, or the manager who does not want a colleague's assistance, a trusted subordinate can help. The use of outside advisors—the company's attorney, accountant, management consultant—are other alternatives.

The job-offer interview should be conducted by the department head or manager to whom the new employee will report.

CHARACTERISTICS OF A GOOD INTERVIEWER

According to a survey of business and personnel managers, the following skills distinguish the outstanding interviewer. The successful interviewer is able to:

1. Put applicants at ease.

2. Make an objective decision despite subjective reactions to the applicant's appearance, personality or background.

3. Understand and empathize with an applicant's fears and anxieties.

4. Make the hiring decision without unnecessary delay.

Once you finish the rest of the chapters in Part III, you should possess these characteristics and more. You'll have augmented your natural interpersonal skills. You'll have learned how veteran interviewers conduct themselves. You'll be more comfortable with the entire process. In short, you'll have developed a proficiency in one of the most crucial managerial skills in the arsenal of any rising executive. Before you get into the interviewing information, there are a couple of preliminary areas to cover, namely salary ranges and job applications.

SALARY RANGES

For every job the company should have a predetermined salary range. Several factors go into determining this range.

The most important of these is the "going rate" for that type of position in the geographical area. This can be ascertained by salary surveys. Some surveys are made by government organizations or trade associations; others are often made by the companies themselves. They obtain the information from other companies in their communities who agree to share their information.

For example, if a firm wants to know what salary range accountants with a certain number of years of experience are being paid, it can ask other firms in the area who hire accountants what the salary ranges are. In return, when the other firm wants to know the salary range for, say, a mechanical engineer, it will feel free to ask. Determining the range for executives or for persons with specialized backgrounds in the firm's own industry is more difficult. This kind of information generally comes from competitors and they may be reluctant to share it. Checking want ads in newspapers is another way to get salary ranges.

The salaries offered should bear some relationship to those being paid to current employees in similar jobs to maintain an equitable balance. If a newcomer is paid more than persons doing similar work, morale suffers. Experience has shown that it is very difficult to maintain secrecy about salaries. The applicant's current compensation and the salary sought also affect what the company will offer.

THE APPLICATION FORM

Where the job specifications describe what to look for in an applicant, the application form lists vital statistics. These include: extent and quality of education, work history (including dates, positions held, employers, a brief description of duties and responsibilities, salary, and reasons for leaving), outstanding achievements, special knowledge. Positions that require special credentials may require specially designed forms.

Chapter 8 dealt with job application forms. Today, many people place more emphasis on the résumé than on the application. That is a mistake; one should complement the other. Résumés supplement applications; they do not replace them.

Before the interview starts, go over both forms. Make notes to ask questions where the information given is insufficient or inconsistent.

SOME TIPS ON READING A RÉSUMÉ

While a résumé can't take the place of an application and interview, it is a vital supplement to the entire selection process. In fact, no management job can be had today without one.

There are reams of literature on how to write a resume. But you're interested in the other side of the coin: how to read one. Here is some advice on that vital selection element.

Since finding the right person for the right job is critical to the success of any organization, the ability to analyze a résumé quickly and correctly has assumed a position of prime importance in the order of priorities for today's busy manager.

As vice president of the highly regarded executive search and management consulting firm of Marshall Consultants, Inc., based in New York City, Judith Cushman had thousands of résumés cross her desk.

Keep the Company
Outlook in Mind

First, Cushman recommends that the businessperson who's eager to hire must have a strong understanding not only of the job to be filled, but also of the organization or department where that individual will work.

Normally each résumé reader will have a specific job in mind, one that demands certain objectives or characteristics in a person. A potential engineer will need one type of background, while a factory foreman will need something entirely different.

"But you must have a picture of the whole department in mind, not just the individual job," asserted Cushman. "For example, you might not want to hire a twenty-five-year-old to work in a group that has nobody under fifty in it, or just the opposite.

"The same idea pertains to style. If you have a department that works on projects that are very team-oriented, you don't want to hire a loner or a person who keeps to him- or herself all the time. They just won't fit in.

"What I'm saying here is that outside factors—such as compatibility, orientation and goals—should be given equal weight with specific job requirements. And the person doing the hiring must therefore have a thorough insight into the organization as well as the job itself."

One way to determine whether an individual's characteristics and behavior will coincide with those of the company is to examine the personal section of the résumé. Hobbies, personal interests and pursuits, and community activities can all provide a revealing insight as to how an individual's personality might mesh with the "personality" of the company.

Study the Career Track

One of the most important reflections of a person's abilities can be assessed by what Cushman refers to as the "career track."

Most employers are interested in a high-potential candidate, but you have to make sure that that potential is being utilized, not wasted. That's where the career track comes into play. Basically, if a person has accepted increasing responsibility with each job movement, and has achieved some amount of success in those posts, he or she can be judged as fulfilling some part of their potential.

There are, of course, several tangible proofs which reflect successful career growth. One obviously is title. Consistent improvement of a person's office from lower-management ranks to higher ones indicates achievement, especially when increasing responsibility accompanies those title changes.

Additional evidence of career improvement is the different types of firms where an applicant has been employed. Graduating from a smaller company to a larger one, or from a nondescript company to a very prestigious one, is also a positive indication of ability.

Money as an Important Measure

While many people contend that money should not be the prime motivating force in job decision-making, it nevertheless does provide the manager studying a recruit's résumé with a good index of success. A solid record of salary achievement indicates that all of the person's former employers judged them successful.

Cushman, however, pointed out two areas to look out for concerning monetary advances. First, they should be significent. If a person earned only "inflation" raises, then the employer didn't consider that individual better than average.

Also, there is a correlation between salary and years of experience. An older worker may be commanding a certain salary only because of age and job-longevity, not because of individual achievement. It's a good idea to keep abreast of industry pay scales before using money as a measurement of individual success.

Recognizing Reputations

The amount of time spent on various jobs is always of paramount importance to any résumé. And prospective employers should always be wary of any "blank spots" in a career picture, or inconsistent movement from one job to another at short time intervals.

But of equal importance are the reputations of the companies where those jobs were held. A good résumé reader will do his or her homework so as to recognize and assess the types of companies that the prospective employee has been working for.

If a person has worked for organizations that command little respect or—even worse—have unsavory reputations, that candidate probably will not possess the solid experience you feel will be needed for the post you have in mind.

Conversely, if the candidate has worked with a progressive or well-respected firm, he or she has probably received the training that you're looking for. The adage about "judging a person by the company he keeps" is especially applicable in this situation.

At the same time, the reputations of a person's former employers can also provide clues to an individual's characteristics. If a company is known for having a leadership that is aggressive and forthright, a successful "graduate" of that company will probably possess those traits.

If your job requires a low-key, low-profile type, you'd be best served by hiring someone coming from an organization with that type of reputation.

A Final Caution:
Direct Contact Is Still Best

"Remember," cautioned Cushman, "that the résumé—no matter how well you read it—is only a word outline of an individual's life.

"And since many are not all that well prepared, a sound final judgment for hiring someone can only be made through direct personal contact.

"But by correctly analyzing a résumé, you'll be able to limit the number of interviews you have to conduct, and save yourself valuable time in the entire job-hiring process."

23

CONDUCTING
THE INTERVIEW

Who should conduct the interview depends on the size of the company and the nature of the job. Some companies have personnel specialists do all the interviewing. Others permit department heads to do their own hiring. Still others have personnel specialists who "screen" applicants, then refer finalists to the department head or senior manager for a second interview and final selection. Candidates for the most important positions are interviewed by a top executive.

The more responsibility you assume and the more people you have under you, the more you'll be called on to utilize your interviewing skills. Now is the time to prepare.

STRUCTURING THE INTERVIEW

Successful interviewers structure a meeting by:

1. Establishing rapport

2. Getting a perspective on the applicant's background

3. Obtaining detailed information about all aspects of an applicant's education and experience

4. Evaluating special accomplishments

5. Evaluating organization ability (for managerial applicants)

6. Evaluating the applicant's potential to fit in the job and the company

7. Evaluating personal characteristics

8. Giving information about the company and the job

9. Allowing the applicant to ask questions

10. Discussing salary.

PHRASING INQUIRIES

All questions, even those designed to get detailed information on specific areas, should be open-ended. A well-phrased query will elicit a descriptive response rather than a yes or no answer. It's better to start with: "Tell me about your job as production supervisor," rather than "Are you now a production supervisor?"

HOW TO USE
NONDIRECTIVE INTERVIEWING

Another means of obtaining information from an applicant is nondirective interviewing. Where in directive (or direct) interviewing, specific questions seek specific information, in nondirective interviewing, applicants are given an opportunity to say what is on their minds. There are few direct questions. A typical *direct* question for the applicant for office manager is: "How many people did you supervise in your last job?" The direct response is followed with additional, more detailed inquiries.

Nondirective questions are open-ended and very broad. They encourage people to tell as much as possible by not channeling the answers. Here's an example of a nondirective question for the office manager applicant: "Tell me about your supervisory experience." You then sit back and listen:

Applicant: I supervised twenty-two people.

Interviewer: (Remains silent)

Applicant: Twelve were women and ten were men.

Interviewer: Mm. (Nodding)

Applicant: I had no trouble with the women, but had a hard time supervising the men.

The nondirective cues—silence, such neutral comments as "okay," "yes," and similar responses—encourage the applicant to continue. The applicant may well tell you things that you might never have had a chance to ask during a direct interview.

However, nondirective interviewing takes too much time to be used throughout every interview. It's greatest use is to obtain supplementary information.

ESTABLISHING RAPPORT

Good rapport depends upon three factors: (1) the way in which the applicant is greeted; (2) the atmosphere of the room in which the interview is held; and (3) the tone set during the opening minutes of the interview.

The first goal of any interviewer is to put the applicant at ease as quickly as possible. You can get off to a good start by personally going to the reception area and greeting the applicant warmly and enthusiastically—and by name.

To be avoided: having your secretary escort the candidate to the office where you're sitting behind your desk reading the applicant's résumé. Intimidation of this kind works against establishing a rapport.

A private office or conference room provides the best setting for an interview. Many managers now interview job applicants in the same place that they interview customers and employees: a corner of their office where comfortable chairs are placed alongside a coffee table. They keep interruptions at a minimum and arrange for telephone calls to be held until the meeting is over.

Open the conversation with relaxed noncontroversial conversation to put the applicant at ease. The traditional areas—weather, travel, sports, recent local events—can be supplemented by any informal ideas you pick up from a reading of the applicant's résumé or application.

Comments about mutual acquaintances or the friend or business associate who referred the applicant provide a smooth way to begin the interview.

The résumé or application offers a good source of information for conversational questions. Showing an interest in one of the applicant's accomplishments or past jobs is flattering and will help put him or her at ease.

DEALING WITH AN APPLICANT'S NERVOUSNESS

One way to overcome an applicant's uneasiness or anxiety (frequently indicated by nervous nods, mumbled monosyllabic comments, taking off and putting on eye-glasses every few minutes) is to mention an experience you may have in common, school, military service, children, hobbies, or professional or trade associations to which both parties may belong. Referring to the applicant's past successes, jobs or other activities listed in the application or résumé is usually effective.

To be avoided: beginning an interview with a question that can be interpreted as a challenge. For example, the question "What makes you think you can handle this job?" will put an applicant on the defensive and probably close off the flow of information. This kind of question should be asked only later in the interview—if at all.

Once the conversation is under way, you can begin to get a sense of what the applicant has done by inquiring about the tasks performed and the responsibilities held in previous positions: "Tell me about a typical day on your last job."

An applicant for office manager might answer: "I was responsible for supervising six clerks and typists, three bookkeepers, and the switchboard operator. I also kept records of all cash transactions, purchased office supplies and equipment, instituted new systems and procedures, and hired all office personnel."

Make notes of those parts of the candidate's response that you want to probe later in the meeting.

DETAILED INFORMATION ON EDUCATION AND EXPERIENCE

One good approach is these five basic questions about school and each job: "What," "When," "Where," "Who," "Why." To complete the background, only "How" need be added:

"*What* skills were needed to accomplish that task?"

"*When* did you do this kind of work?"

"*Where* was this applicable?"

"*Who* was responsible?"

"*Why* did you make that decision?"

"*How* did you solve this problem?"

As a general rule, it is unproductive to spend time on the educational background of people who have been out of school for a number of years. (How to interview recent graduates is discussed in Chapter 26.) A few minutes to verify degrees and technical courses is adequate.

The example below shows how asking the same probing questions of two applicants for the office manager's job elicits answers that help you as the interviewer to decide which is the superior candidate:

Interviewer:
On what basis did you assign work to your subordinates?

Applicant A:
I knew each of their capabilities and passed out the work accordingly.

Interviewer:
How did you make sure that the work was being done properly?

Interviewer:
On what basis did you assign work to your subordinates?

Applicant B:
I divided my people into four sections and each section was responsible for a specific portion of the work.

Interviewer:
How did you make sure that the work was being done properly?

Applicant A:
I checked all the work myself.

Interviewer:
Wasn't this very time-consuming?

Applicant A:
It was my job and I did it.

Interviewer:
How did you find the time?

Applicant A:
This took most of my day and often I had to work into the evening.

Applicant B:
All work was logged in when completed. Critical areas were checked regularly.

Interviewer:
How effective was this?

Applicant B:
Errors were minimal and it gave me time to attend to other things.

Interviewer:
For example?

Applicant B:
Planning, developing new systems, etc.

This close questioning revealed that Applicant B is much more systematic and effective than Applicant A.

Another series of questions probes supervisory abilities:

Interviewer:
What methods did you use to appraise people's work?

Applicant A:
We had no formal system. If they did poorly I let them know it.

Interviewer:
What methods did you use to appraise people's work?

Applicant B:
The company did not have a formal system, but I would sit down with my people periodically and review their work.

Interviewer:
What if they were doing well?

Applicant A:
I praised good performance, but I reserved this for really outstanding work.

Interviewer:
When promotions or raises were requested, on what basis did you make your decision?

Applicant A:
I knew which people were doing well and which were doing badly and I'd make recommendations based on that knowledge.

Interviewer:
On what basis?

Applicant B:
We set up standards for every phase of each job and each person knew what was expected of him or her. We talked about how well they were meeting these expectations. If they were not being met, we discussed what they could do to improve their work.

Interviewer:
When promotions or raises were requested, on what basis did you make your decision?

Applicant B:
Those persons who met their goals on a regular basis received raises automatically. Promotions were given on the basis of exceptional performance and capability for handling whatever higher position they were qualified for.

Similar questions should be asked for every phase of the job. They are derived from the job description, prior consultation with the supervisor of the job, personal knowledge of the job, or written material describing job functions. The following are useful questions for technical, administrative, and professional applicants (tips for interviewing for supervisory positions appear in Chapter 26):

1. To determine the applicant's ability to innovate and adapt to change: "How did you change the content of your job from the time when you assumed it until now?"

2. To find out about strengths and weaknesses: "For what things have your immediate superiors complimented you? Criticized you?"

3. To evaluate current readiness to perform the job now open: "If you were doing this job, in what areas could you contribute immediately? Where would you need added training?"

A CHECKLIST OF INTERVIEW QUESTIONS

The following checklist will give you a good idea of what professional interviewers use as the basis for their questioning.

Selection Interview Questions:

1. What would you say are some of your most significant accomplishments? Include operating results and any other accomplishments you consider important.

2. What do you think is behind your success?

3. Were there any unusual difficulties you had to overcome?

4. What did you particularly like about the position?

5. What would you say you liked least about the position?

6. What responsibilities or results did not come up to your expectations?

7. What would you say you learned on your last job?

8. What planning processes have you found useful and how do you go about them?

9. In what way do you feel you have improved in your planning activity in the last few years?

10. Describe how you went about making important types of decisions or recommendations.

11. What types of decisions are easiest for you to make and which ones are difficult?

12. What's the biggest business mistake you can recall?

13. In what respects do you feel you have improved in your decision-making?

14. How do you think your subordinates would describe you as a delegator?

15. What pattern of organization do you follow? How has it changed in the last few years?

16. What has been the most upsetting surprise you have suffered when something was getting out of control?

17. What things do you think contribute to your effectiveness as a supervisor? What do you think are your weakest points as an effective supervisor?

18. In what respects do you feel you have improved most as a supervisor during the last few years?

19. What have you done about your own skill development in the last few years?

20. Describe your relationship with your last three supervisors.

21. Describe one or two innovations you are particularly proud of.

22. How do you feel about your progress (career-wise) to date?

23. What are your aspirations for the future and how have they changed?

24. What would you say are your main assets, your strengths, and what would you say are your limitations?

SPECIAL ACCOMPLISHMENTS

Future expectations rest at least partly on past performance. A superior prospect generally has significant past accomplishments. To reveal just how significant the achievement is, the initial question, "What do you consider to be your most significant accomplishment?" can be followed by more probing inquiries.

For instance, if the applicant answers: "I introduced a system that cut costs 10 percent," you follow up with: "Describe the original system," "What changes did you make in it?" "What problems did you have putting those changes into effect?" "How did you solve them?" "What were the results?" "How did you measure the savings?"

If a prior job did not lend itself to creativity, or a previous superior stifled initiative, indications of outstanding ability may be found only in outside activities.

Talents applied to educational, civic, religious, trade or professional association activities could—if channeled into work life—make an exceptional employee.

EVALUATING ORGANIZATIONAL ABILITY

For jobs requiring administrative skills, the applicant's ability to manage time and organize work is crucial.

For example:

Interviewer:
How do you organize your day?

Applicant A:
My job is so complex. I can't really plan a day.

Interviewer:
How do you organize your day?

Applicant B:
Every afternoon before I leave for the day, I set up

Problems are always coming up and I have to be flexible if I'm going to solve them. I arrive early and the phone starts ringing. Between handling the daily problems and checking the work, I'm kept busy all day.

Interviewer:

What do you do about matters you can't get to because of unexpected problems?

Applicant A:

I'm not afraid to work long hours to get things done.

Interviewer:

Is there any part of the work you can delegate to others?

Applicant A:

There are some things I can delegate, but since I have to check everything anyway, sometimes it's easier if I do it myself.

a plan for the next day. I list things that must be done in order of importance. I follow my plan as best I can. Of course, if problems come up I have to alter my plans. But by taking care of top priorities first, I make sure they get done no matter what happens.

Interviewer:

What do you do about those matters you can't get to?

Applicant B:

Some can wait for a later time. Others I delegate.

Interviewer:

What do you delegate?

Applicant B:

Each of my people has special knowledge of various aspects of the work, and I give out the assignments accordingly. I also encourage people to take on special projects so that they have these skills when I need them. I discovered that one important by-product of my doing this is that it makes people more promotable.

Other questions that explore organizational ability include:

1. "What responsibility did you have for planning?" "Give some examples of plans you were involved in during the past year."

2. "What decisions could you make without approval from your superiors?" If the applicant has made decisions on personnel, purchasing or other important matters, ask for specific examples.

3. "What would it have cost the company if you had made a poor decision?" (Asking about its monetary impact is a good way to evaluate the importance of the applicant's role.)

To find out if the applicant approaches problems systematically, he or she should be asked to explain, in detail, how they devised a particular solution, and the reasons for selecting one approach over another at each step. This will show you not only what they did but how they think.

24

MATCHING
THE EMPLOYEE WITH
THE COMPANY

A good fit requires a congruence between what the applicant seeks and what the job and company have to offer. A mismatch may lead to dissatisfaction, demoralization, and early resignation. These questions help determine how well the applicant will fit into the job and the company:

"What are you seeking in this job that you are not getting in your present one?"

"What do you want to avoid in your next job that bothers you now?" If the same problems exist in the job to be filled as in the applicant's current job, it is a poor fit.

Example: The applicant who objects to being away from home would not be suitable for a job which requires extensive travel.

"Why are you seeking a job at this time?" The reason for being in the job market may tell a great deal abut the applicant. A typical pat response, such as "limited growth in my current job" sounds convincing, but is really ambiguous and requires further explanation. While this answer could indicate ambition, it may also show impatience or unrealistic expectations, particularly if the person has been on that present job only a short time.

If the job calls for someone who will eventually move up in the organization, you should listen for an expressed desire to advance and a willingness to work hard. Some good questions to ask are:

"Why are you interested in this type of career?"

"What are your long-term career objectives?"

"How do you plan to reach your goals?"

"What goals did you set for yourself in your last job? How close did you come to reaching them?"

Applicants who have career objectives should be able to describe them, to show enthusiasm about reaching them, and to report on what they have done to attain goals in the past.

PERSONAL CHARACTERISTICS

The following is a list of personal qualities essential to the performance of most technical, administrative, and professional jobs:

Intelligence.   What *kind* of intelligence is needed for the job? If the job calls for someone who can think fast under pressure, you might look for rapid responses to questions. If the job calls for deliberative, analytical thinking, quick answers to complex questions are a bad sign. Problem-solving intelligence is best determined by posing questions that test the applicant's logic.

For younger applicants, grades attained in the university or schools attended indicate at least a conceptual intelligence. If grades were poor, you should try to learn if there were any extenuating circumstances.

Energy level. In addition to observing whether the applicant responds rapidly and firmly, you might ask: "What types of recreational activities do you engage in? What are you doing to keep physically fit?"

People who engage in sports or have a regimen of physical fitness are more likely to have a higher level of energy.

Maturity. Questions that might determine an applicant's maturity are:

"What personal goals (other than business) have you set for yourself?" Mature people usually have more realistic goals for themselves and their families.

"What was the most important decision you had to make in the past five years? Tell me how you reached this decision." It could be a business or personal decision. The answers will certainly reflect the applicant's maturity and judgment.

"If you were to start your career again, what changes would you make?" The response should show not only maturity, but the applicant's attitude toward work. In other words, if the applicant is interested in a career that differs markedly from the job for which he or she is being interviewed, you'll find out PDQ.

Resourcefulness. Some people capably tackle all kinds of challenges—an important trait for those assuming positions of responsibility.

Good questions for probing resourcefulness include:

"What were some of the more difficult problems you encountered on your last job? How did you solve them?"

"To whom did you go for counsel when you couldn't handle a problem on the job? Give me some examples."

Leadership. For a management position, not only leadership ability, but the right management style is essential. Since styles range from autocratic to permissive, the important thing is that the applicant's and company's styles do not conflict.

For instance:

Interviewer:
When you got a rush job, how did you get people to meet the deadline?

Applicant A:
I told them what to do and they did it. They knew who the boss was.

Interviewer:
How did that work?

Applicant A:
They grumbled, but the work was usually done on time.

Interviewer:
When you got a rush job, how did you get people to meet the deadline?

Applicant B:
I brought them together, explained the job and impressed on them the importance of meeting the deadline. I then asked if they had any suggestions to get the work done on time.

Interviewer:
How did that work?

Applicant B:
We worked as a team and my people really produced. We usually met our time commitments.

Interviewer:
How much turnover did you have in your department?

Applicant A:
You know how these clerks and typists are. To them it's just a job, so we had the usual turnover.

Interviewer:
How was the turnover in your department?

Applicant B:
Very low. Our people rarely left except for the usual personal reasons: pregnancy, relocation to another part of the country, etc. It was about 8 percent a year.

Interviewer:
What was the percentage?

Applicant A:
About 30 percent each year.

These answers give a good picture of the two applicants' leadership styles. Here are additional questions to ask: "What type of other 'people-problems' did you encounter? Give some examples and describe what you did to solve them." This will enable you to judge the applicants' capabilities in interpersonal relationships.

Those with little or no managerial experience in previous jobs may have shown potential for it elsewhere. They should be asked about leadership in school, societies, community, or other activities.

Common mistake: hiring or promoting someone into management purely on the basis of technical competence; the best salesperson is made the sales manager; the superior mechanic is promoted to foreman; a competent engineer is hired as engineering manager. It requires special characteristics to manage. Fortunately, some people have both managerial and technical abilities.

Assertiveness. Sample questions:

"What was the most novel, unusual or innovative idea you introduced in your company? How did you persuade management to accept this idea?"

"In committee work or team projects, what part did you play?"

"Give some examples of situations where you had to convince other members of a group to see things your way."

Ability to work under direction. Answers to the following questions will show how the applicant responds to and carries out orders:
"Describe each of your former managers' supervisory methods. Evaluate them." This shows what type of leadership the applicant responds to best. The style of management the applicant works well with should match that of the person to whom he or she will report. If it differs significantly, it may augur problems.

Attitudes. How a prospective employee feels about work is as important as how that work is done. Does the employee see it as enforced drudgery required to make a living, or as something from which to gain satisfaction? This can be determined by asking: "What did you like best (least) about your job? In what activities are you engaged outside of work?"
Most jobs don't require total dedication. But for those

in management and professional jobs, excessive outside interests may indicate that the applicant looks for self-fulfillment off the job.

Communication ability.   If the job calls for giving speeches or representing the company to others, ask about experience in these areas and then listen to how clear and concise the answers are.

To evaluate written communication skills, the applicant may be asked to write a letter after the interview concerning some specific problem that might be faced on the job. The way the ideas are expressed in the letter will be as important as the ideas themselves.

GIVING INFORMATION

One of the most important parts of the interview is to give information to the applicant about the company and the job. While you are evaluating the applicants to determine their qualifications, the applicants are evaluating the company and the job. Don't tell a great deal about the job early in the interview because an astute applicant will use the information to tailor responses to questions. For example, if you say that a certain aspect of work is very important, the applicant may exaggerate appropriate parts of his or her background.

However, you must give certain basic information about the job to help determine quickly whether the applicant is interested in that type of work. For example, the supervisor interviewing for the office manager position described earlier might state: "This job requires someone to manage three sections: customer service, office services, and mail and supply services." Only after you are satisfied that the candidate is worth considering for the position—which is usually not until after a later interview—are details given.

General information about the company can be provided at any time during the interview procedure. Some organizations give all applicants copies of brochures describing the company, its products or services, and its history. Once an applicant is being seriously considered, additional information may be provided, such as sales figures (if not confidential), copies of the annual report (if it is a public company) and organization charts showing where the open job fits in relation to the overall management hierarchy. This information can be supplemented by a brief discussion of the company and its place in the industry. For example: "Our company is twenty-five years old. We are now tenth in size in our industry and expect to be in the top five as soon as our new plant is in operation"; or "We have increased our share of the market each year for the past ten years and are working hard to maintain this growth."

"SELLING" THE COMPANY

To insure that a job offer will be accepted, it may be necessary to "sell" the company, particularly if candidates are in a job category that is hard to fill or if they are likely to have other offers. Overselling, however, is a mistake. Exaggerated prospects, false promises or even overly optimistic statements may backfire if the promises or prospects do not materialize.

You should not withhold negative aspects of the organization since the applicants will at some time find out about them. The later they find out, the greater their resentment is likely to be. The resentment could lead to rejection of the job when offered, or, if the person becomes an employee, real bitterness.

When the time comes to discuss the job itself, a good way to start is to have the applicant read the position description (see Part I). You can elaborate on it and answer questions. Among the things that should be discussed are job functions, reporting relationships, special responsibilities, normal work hours, what additional time is expected of the employee, special problems concerning the job, and other pertinent matters. If there is a usual career path from that position up the ladder of the company, this should be explained. An excellent means of assuring that the applicants understand what the job is about is to allow them to observe the job. This is done only with applicants in whom the company has a serious interest. Where feasible, the applicants should be given the opportunity to talk with the incumbent or others in the department, spend several hours or even an entire workday with the people doing the job. This can be followed up with a question-and-answer period with the department head in which other specific matters concerning the job functions can be covered.

ALLOWING THE APPLICANT TO ASK QUESTIONS

Encouraging job candidates to ask questions gives them a chance to obtain information that you may not have provided. The type and depth of information the applicants seek gives you another means of evaluating them. Applicants who ask vague questions about the company or job or show their chief interest in personal benefits—vacations, holidays, salary-review policies—may be less promising. Those with more to offer generally ask about:

- Details of the job

- Technical matters related to the job

- Training offered on the job
- Plans the company has for growth

An applicant who doesn't have any questions can still be prompted. You might say:

> "If you were to start work in our company, what are some of the things about the job you would want to know immediately?"

> "I've asked you a number of questions about your background, attitudes and goals. Do you have any questions about our company's attitudes and goals?"

DISCUSSING SALARY

General discussions about salary should take place well before an offer is made. Most people are given a moderate increase over current salary when they are hired for a new job. Occasionally, there is a good reason for a higher increment, such as improved credentials, an advanced degree or a license that the candidate received to practice a profession since he or she was hired for their last job.

Sometimes applicants are unrealistic about what they believe they can obtain. It is usually inadvisable to upgrade a salary range, particularly if it has been established by careful study. On the other hand, if this person is the only possible candidate who can fill the job, it may be necessary to do this. Clearly stating the facts as the company sees them can offer a strong, but flexible negotiating position.

Applicant: "I would like $20,000, and I think I deserve it."

Interviewer: "In your current job you are earning $15,000. This would be an increase of 33⅓ percent. Most people obtain less than 20 percent, often only 10 percent increases by changing jobs."

Applicant: "I could work for less if the opportunity was there for me to reach $20,000 in a reasonable period of time."

Here you might ask why the person feels he or she deserves more. If satisfied with the response, explain company policy on salary review.

WORKING OUT DIFFERENCES

If an applicant wants more money than the company is willing to pay, aspects of the job can be used to persuade him or her to reconsider. The benefits program or opportunities for growth may outweigh salary considerations. If the applicant has indicated during the interview a special interest in some phase of company business or other needs that the company can meet, these can be emphasized.

Interviewer: "Your salary requirement is higher than we can pay for this job, but you mentioned earlier in the interview your desire to move into a management position. This job is the first rung of a career ladder that most of our managers have climbed. Opportunity for moving into more responsible management positions in relatively short periods of time has been a policy of this company."

Many managers do not like to haggle with applicants about salary and prefer a "take it or leave it" approach. It is not always good policy to negotiate once an offer is made. In any event, salary discrepancies should be resolved *before* offers are made. Problems concerning remuneration should be openly discussed once there is serious interest in an applicant. If they cannot be resolved, an offer should not be made. There are exceptions, of course. Sometimes an applicant has agreed tentatively to a salary, but then receives a higher offer from another company. If the applicant is very desirable, the offer will have to be readjusted.

25

EVALUATING
APPLICANTS

To make systematic evaluations of applicants, you can use an interview summary sheet, such as the two-page form shown in Exhibit 18.

THE INTERVIEW SUMMARY SHEET

"Job factors," duties, responsibilities, aptitudes and skills taken from both the job specifications and job description, are listed in the upper left-hand column. The applicant's qualifications are listed on the right, opposite each factor. The second sheet is used to comment on the applicant's personal characteristics and to summarize his or her strengths and weaknesses.

Only key facets of the applicant's responses are jotted down. You can use the interview summary sheet for the notes. Additional facts or figures that you want to verify later may be noted separately. Taking notes helps to struc-

EXHIBIT 18

An Interview Summary Sheet

Applicant_____   Date_____

Position applied for_____   Interviewer_____

Job factors[1]	Applicant's background[2]
Duties:_____	
Skills required:_____	
Education required:[3] (level)_____	
Specific types:_____	
Educ. achievement:_____	

Other job factors:_____ _____

1. Job factors should be listed from job specifications for position applicant applies for.
2. Interviewer should note aspects of applicant's background that apply to each factor in this column.
3. Level of education—how much schooling completed; type represents subjects related to job taken; achievement represents grades or standing.

Personal factors   **Comments**

   Growth in career ____

   Accomplishments ____

Intangibles ____

   Appearance ____

   Motivation ____

   Resourcefulness ____

   Stability ____

   Leadership ____

   Creativity ____

   Mental alertness ____

   Energy level ____

   Communication skill ____

   Self-confidence ____

Comments

Applicant's strengths:_____

_____

_____

Applicant's limitations:_____

_____

☐ Applicant should be hired._____

  Recommendations for additional training:_____

_____

☐ Applicant should not be hired._____

  Reasons:_____

Additional Comments:_____

---

ture the interview, allows you to keep track of material you want to inquire about without interrupting the applicant at a particular moment and helps you to remember the applicant more clearly after the meeting.

Comparing Qualifications to Job Factors

Where comparisons between the job factors and the applicant's qualifications reveal specific weaknesses, the interviewer may look for compensating experience. For example, although a person does not have a degree in business administration, he or she may have taken seminars on business subjects. While there may be no experience in supervising through subordinate managers, there may be a good background in direct supervision.

Where there are several candidates for a job, summary sheets are compared. Some candidates may be eliminated on the basis of job factors alone.

Since comments on personal characteristics are based on the whole interview, they are written after it is over. This avoids comments based on a first impression.

Evaluating Intangibles

Only those intangible aspects of an applicant's background that are related to the job should be weighed. For example, if the job requires only technical expertise and knowledge—and offers little chance of advancement into management—lack of ambition may be irrelevant. Similarly, a poor grasp of technical concepts may have no bearing on an office manager's job.

You should review the applicant's accomplishments in light of company needs: The higher the level of performance required, the more important an applicant's special achievements in past jobs, school, or outside activities become.

Interviewers, consciously or unconsciously, make a variety of judgments about applicants. For example, inexperienced interviewers tend to overvalue appearance and personal charm. Any unconscious bias may lead to the selection of a less-capable candidate. The best way to avoid basing decisions on personal predilection is to be aware of them. For example, any interviewer who tends to link incompetence with, say, overweight, must go through the mental exercise of remembering that weight has no bearing on the performance of technical, administrative, and professional jobs.

The "Halo" and "Pitchfork" Effects

Another kind of bias is attributing great ability to an applicant because of one outstanding trait. For example, an interviewer may be so impressed by an applicant's grasp of marketing that he or she mistakenly assumes the person to be outstanding in management, finance, and other areas. Psychologists call this the "halo effect" because placing a mental halo over the applicant influences one's judgment of the total person. The opposite of the "halo effect" is the "pitchfork effect." Here the interviewer projects a single weakness into general incompetence.

Sometimes an interviewer will dislike an applicant without knowing why. Perhaps there is an unconscious association of the applicant with an unpleasant person or experience. When an interviewer cannot explain a negative feeling about an applicant who is otherwise qualified for a position, someone else in the organization should interview that applicant. A second opinion may prevent rejection of a potentially valuable asset to the company.

FINAL EVALUATION

When you're making the final hiring decision, you must evaluate candidates' long-range potential in light of the opportunities the company can offer. You may want to select the applicant who has the potential for higher positions even though other candidates are more qualified for the current opening.

For example, one person may fit the current office manager opening. But the company may want to consider a less-qualified candidate who has, for instance, considerable knowledge about computer technology which may be important to the company's future plans. Conversely, some candidates who are well qualified for the current position may lack the education, experience (or interest in) higher-level jobs.

Every manager who interviews an applicant should complete an interview summary sheet and make a hiring recommendation. Each interviewer's recommendations should be considered along with information from references and other sources.

When lower-level managers perform screening interviews for you, they may use a simplified "Screening Interview Summary" such as that shown in Exhibit 19.

Any reservations about qualifications must be discussed with the applicant *before* any offer is made. For example, if the applicant does not have experience in budgeting, but has an overall background that would qualify him or her for the job, an offer might be conditional upon the applicant's agreement to take courses in budgeting or learn it on the job. The condition should be discussed fully with the applicant until it is clearly understood and agreed upon.

CREATING AN INTERVIEW REPORT

Whether you eventually decide to hire a person or not, you should keep a file report on each candidate that you interview. This is not only good business practice, but helps fulfill EEO requirements. By maintaining a record of the reasons for hiring or rejecting applicants, you also anticipate the possibility that they will turn up at a later date and go through the whole process with someone else.

EXHIBIT 19

A Screening Interview Summary Sheet

Applicant's Name_____Job Applied For_____

Interviewer's Name_____Interviewer's Title_____

Directions: Obtain a copy of the job specifications and the job description before holding the interview. If they are not available, obtain job specifications, duties and responsibilities, and special working conditions from the appropriate department head or senior executive.

	Unac-ceptable	Accep-table	Out-standing	Com-ments
1. Does applicant have basic education for the job?				
2. Does applicant have basic experience for the job?				
3. Does applicant have special skills required for the job?				
4. Can applicant meet special working conditions required				
5. Is grooming and general appearance adequate for job?				

6. Does applicant
   show enthusiasm
   and interest in the
   work?
   _____

7. Does applicant
   communicate well?
   (Evaluate only if
   needed for job.)
   _____

Overall rating of applicant_____

Length of Interview_____

Recommend for further consideration_____

Date_____

Many professional interviewers use dictating equipment to prepare their reports. Your company's personnel people may currently employ this technique. Since you probably don't do a lot of interviewing at this juncture of your career, you may not need such apparatus. But it does come in handy if you've done several interviews and want to separate out distinct reactions to the job candidates.

Whether you use a recording device or not, just the act of completing an interview report is helpful. It will crystallize your thinking, help you compare and contrast candidates, and make your decision-making more logical and objective.

Different interviewers approach the written report in different ways. Some prefer a very rigid, formal outline to fill in, one with boxes to check and numbers to develop as summary judgments. Others opt for a more freewheeling style, a stream-of-consciousness reaction to the overall interview. You should adapt a review form that fits your style and that of your company. A couple of ingredients are essential, though.

For one, you should make lists of the candidates' strong and weak points as you see them vis-à-vis the job in question. Intelligence, technical ability, leadership qualities, motivational outlook, interpersonal skills, level of work standards, etc., should all be included.

After you've set your sketch comparison of the strengths/ weaknesses, develop an overall summary. Here you can elaborate on how you think the candidate would work out as an employee; where the strengths outweigh the weaknesses and vice versa.

Make sure you tie in all your evaluations and judgments to the specific job the candidate is being interviewed for. And make just as sure that he or she will fit into your company's style and employee work force.

26

SPECIAL
INTERVIEWING PROBLEMS

Probably the greatest challenge to an interviewer is applicants who have just completed their formal educations. How can a manager determine if the candidate is worth investing the time and money that will be needed for training? The answer is that you must get the applicant to reveal past patterns of behavior—since these are likely to continue in the next position—and you must evaluate his or her knowledge of the job applied for.

EVALUATING PAST
BEHAVIOR PATTERNS

To evaluate motivational patterns the following selected questions can elicit information on different kinds of behavior: "What were your ambitions when you were in school?" "What positions of leadership did you attain?" "How successful were you in achieving the goals of the groups you headed?" "What are your career or professional goals?" "What are you doing to help achieve them?" Highly motivated people have goals. And they strive to reach them early in their lives. Students generally manifest this trait through active participation in school activities.

Situational questions are helpful for people who have not had experience in a specific field. You can ask applicants how they might handle simulated situations they may meet on the job. The following is an example of a situational question about a customer service job.

Question: "A customer is irate about a delayed shipment from your firm. How would you handle this complaint?"

Poor response: "I'd apologize for the delay and report it to the shipping department for action."

Better response: "I'd apologize for the delay and tell the customer I'd check into its status and let them know when they can expect delivery—and that I would do what I could to personally expedite it."

Situational questions can be developed for every type of position.

To evaluate work patterns: "How did you organize your time?" "How did you approach reports that you had to prepare?"

Personal or intangible characteristics can be measured as described earlier: intelligence by grade level or class standing, initiative by extracurricular school activities, creativity by questions about hobbies, special projects or papers that the applicant feels show inventiveness.

EVALUATING GENERAL JOB KNOWLEDGE

This may be ascertained with a straightforward question: "How do you view the job for which you are applying?" If the applicant is applying for a position as a marketing trainee, he or she should have a basic concept of what a marketing job entails. Although the applicant may not be able to describe the job itself, an answer will show whether or not an understanding exists about the kind of work involved. For example:

Interviewer: "How do you view the job of a marketing assistant?"

Poor response: "I assume I would be helping the marketing manager handle details of that job."

Better response: "A marketing assistant would help prepare studies of customers' needs, analyze trends in various markets and assist in handling customer relations. Perhaps after training, it might involve making complete market surveys."

A good follow-up question: "What have you studied that would help you succeed in this type of work?" Some applicants may have studied specific subjects that prepared them for the job. If they have, they should be questioned about the subjects taken, papers written, projects in which they participated.

If an applicant's education was not specific, you can probe for useful skills that may have been acquired.

To probe research skills: "What projects did you engage in that required research? Describe one in detail."

To probe public speaking: "What opportunities have you had to speak before groups? Tell me about some of them."

EXPERIENCE IN OTHER FIELDS

Some applicants have good experience, but in a different type of business. For example, an applicant for the office manager's position may have supervised a credit department. After developing rapport with the applicant, you can

ask, as you did the person without experience, "How do
you view the job of an office manager?"

This should be followed with, "What in your past experience or training will help you become successful in this
job?"

Poor response: "I can do anything I set out to do. I'm
a fast learner."

Better response: "As a credit manager, I managed a
staff of twelve people. I hired, trained, and directed these
people. In addition, I developed systems and procedures
which expedited the work."

People whose experience was in a different type of work
should be asked for specific examples of their duties and
accomplishments. You should analyze how the applicant
achieved results rather than what kind of work he or she
did. Here, too, situational questions are useful.

INTERVIEWING FOR A SUPERVISORY POSITION

As you attain levels in the corporate hierarchy, you'll have
more people reporting to you and more hiring decisions to
make. And the level of the employee will rise as well. At
this time you may be more involved in selecting lower-level
employees, but eventually you'll have supervisory and managerial positions to fill.

Once you have determined what a particular supervisory
job will require (see Part I), you should review these requirements in the broader context of personal characteristics. You might find it helpful to draw up a list of what you
consider to be the "ideal" attributes of a supervisor.

Obviously, no single candidate is going to be "ideal."
But those whose attitudes and approaches to the work em-

body the following qualities are more likely to succeed. The specific problems or demands of your own company will necessitate adding categories to the list:

- *Enthusiasm for the work.* This involves personal motivation to achieve and to succeed. Most people like the idea of getting a higher salary, but that in itself isn't enough. Becoming a supervisor means taking on more responsibility. The person who will accept responsibility willingly, and with genuine enthusiasm, is the one you're looking for.

- *The ability to motivate others.* An effective supervisor is able to transmit enthusiasm to the workers; he or she knows what is needed to motivate them. Watch the natural leaders in your department and you'll see this characteristic in action.

- *Respect of co-workers.* It is better, of course, to have a supervisor who is liked rather than disliked, but here you want something more than popularity. In fact, popularity has a way of fading when an individual is promoted over other co-workers. But respect—fostered by honesty, fairness, and the courage to make decisions and stick by them—is more abiding.

- *Sensitivity toward others.* To be effective, a supervisor must understand human relations. Being able to put that understanding to good use is even more important. A supervisor has to be able to spot signs of discontent and deal with them before real trouble breaks out.

- *Technical know-how.* The specifics on this point will be determined by the type of department to be supervised. Your job analysis and job description should tell you what to look for. However, this factor doesn't necessarily mean promoting your best line worker. Technical know-how alone won't be enough if the candidate doesn't meet the other requirements as well. A supervisor's job is to get the work done through others.

Balance among these attributes is the key to picking the right candidate. Look for the person in whom your "ideal" attributes appear in proportion to each other and to the demands of the job.

ATTITUDES TOWARD JOB AND PERFORMANCE TO LOOK FOR

In judging supervisory job candidates, it's often helpful to have a list of specific questions requiring concrete, detailed answers to guide your evaluations. The answers to any of these questions can give you extra insight:

1. Does the employee accept supervision readily—with a desire to improve performance?

2. Does the employee approach his or her present work with enthusiasm?

3. Does the employee cooperate willingly?

4. Barring unforeseen circumstances, can the individual be relied on to meet work deadlines? Work well within schedules which are set? Pace the work without a formal schedule? Or need close supervision?

5. Does the person plan the work before starting, or try to organize while working?

6. Does the candidate understand the importance of the work and how it fits in the total scheme of things?

7. Does the candidate's performance indicate concern with more than just doing his or her job? Does he or she consider how individual actions affect the work of others?

8. Does the person volunteer for additional work and responsibility?

9. Does the prospective supervisor accept changes in procedures readily or resist them?

10. Does the candidate devise and suggest new work methods?

11. Does the candidate understand and comply with company policies and regulations?

27

COMMON
INTERVIEWING
MISTAKES AND
PROBLEM APPLICANTS

There are six common interviewing mistakes:

1. Telegraphing expected answers to the applicant. The interviewer lets the applicant know, directly or indirectly, what he or she wants. Rhetorical questions such as "You have experience in cost accounting, don't you?" elicit a "yes" even if the applicant's experience is minimal.

2. Intimidating the applicant. This can cut off all substantive communication. Typical examples of intimidating actions include: keeping an applicant waiting for an unreasonably long time; using a hostile tone of voice; asking threatening questions; setting traps to catch inconsistencies. Some interviewers deliberately use these tactics to test stamina. They want to see if the applicant will be able to take pressure on the job. Such tactics, part of the "stress interviewing" technique, rarely succeed. The applicants who survive may be tough, but

the interviewer may still not know whether they can do the job.

3. Talking too much. Many interviewers spend too much time talking about the job, the company, or themselves, effectively preventing the applicant from giving vital information.

4. Taking too many notes. Although notes are important, writing too much during an interview is distracting and can inhibit the flow of information from the applicant.

5. Using technical vocabulary with nontechnical applicants. While using accepted terminology is a good way to test technical applicants' knowledge of their trade, it should be avoided with others. Interviewers with engineering or other technical experience have a tendency to forget the applicant's background.

6. Failing to listen properly. Perhaps the most important recommendation for good interviewing is to LISTEN. Contrary to popular belief, this requires an *overt* effort. A good way to maintain concentration is to focus on the applicant's facial expressions and other nonverbal behavior.

PROBLEM APPLICANTS

While you can work to improve your interviewing technique, there are some problems over which you have little control: those created by the applicant. They may be good applicants who simply interview badly. Or they may have problems that would make it unwise to hire them. Here are some examples of problem applicants:

The overly talkative applicant. Answers every question with a dissertation. Asked what time it is, responds by telling how to build a clock. As bad an impression as this makes, it may just be nervousness that hides real talent. However, you may need to interrupt frequently with specific questions. Some applicants may be glib or may tell one story after another to mask their lack of qualifications. With a little patience, you will be able to discern the good from the unqualified.

The reluctant applicant. To overcome reluctance, often caused by anxiety, more time must be spent developing rapport. Again, talking about noncontroversial matters or complimenting the applicant on some aspect of his or her background can help. Once the applicant is relaxed and talking freely, the interviewer can get into details.

The belligerent applicant. Typically tries to put the interviewer on the defensive and may even try to force the interviewer into an argument on a specific qualification. Generally such applicants should not be hired. Experienced interviewers remain calm at all times and never allow themselves to get into an argument. They keep the initiative and end the interview diplomatically, but as quickly as possible.

The high-pressure applicant. Such applicants may describe other offers received, chiefly from competitors, and try to show that if the interviewer doesn't make a favorable decision immediately the company will lose a sure winner. Pressed for details of accomplishments, they usually respond with vague comments—but no specifics. They may try to persuade the interviewer that, although their experience is slight, they can do the job if given the chance.

28

OTHER APPROACHES
TO INTERVIEWING

There are two basic ways to vary the interviewing process: one is to alter the number of interviews an applicant goes through; the other is to change the format of the interview itself. The sequential and serialized interviews are multiple interviewing techniques. They offer the company more than one view of the applicant. The panel and structured interviews, by altering the format, offer you a different method of inquiry.

SEQUENTIAL INTERVIEWS

This is the most commonly used technique. Applicants are screened by a lower-ranking person in the company. If they are considered worthy of further consideration, they are passed on to you or the next highest-ranking person who interviews them and decides whether to pass them on—or hire them for themselves.

This procedure eliminates unqualified people before they take a senior manager's valuable time. Sometimes, two or more lower-level interviewers compare evaluations and choose a few top applicants for final interviews with a department head or one of the members of top-level management.

THE SERIALIZED INTERVIEW

In this system the personnel department (or an administrative assistant), screens out the obviously unqualified candidates according to specific guidelines. All candidates who meet the basic qualifications are interviewed by at least two other company representatives. They may be personnel specialists, the department head, or other members of the department that has the job opening.

No one interviewer can reject anyone. Each interviewer completes a summary sheet for each applicant. When all interviews are completed, the interviewers meet, compare summary sheets and decide which candidates to present to the department manager for the final decision.

The serialized interview enables the manager to whom the new employee will report to base that decision on the perspectives and evaluations of many managers. Different interviewers may uncover different facts or temper one another's biases, increasing the chances for a wise hiring decision. The procedure's greatest limitation is that it is time consuming, expensive, and—depending upon the availability of those designated to interview—difficult to schedule. This may lead to delays in filling the position and the loss of good candidates who decide to accept positions elsewhere.

THE PANEL INTERVIEW

Instead of having each of the company representatives interview the applicant separately, a group of managers interview the applicant at the same time. It is usually conducted as a conference, with one of the panelists acting as chairman. After developing rapport, the panelists ask questions. They follow no pattern; questions are unplanned—spontaneous. Follow-up inquiries may come from different panel members.

After the interview, the panel discusses the candidate and decides to hire, not hire, or delay its decision until it has seen other applicants.

The panel interview minimizes the time managers must take from regular duties, allows all interviewers to base comments and comparisons on a uniform experience, and increases the chances that questions missed by one interviewer will be asked by another.

Potential Problems

Some applicants are intimidated by panel interviews and may not respond well. This can be offset to some degree by briefing the candidate in advance concerning the purpose of the panel interview: to give a number of managers an efficient means of exchanging ideas with the applicant about the job. The applicant should also be informed in advance who will sit on the panel. It is inadvisable to use this technique in a first interview. The applicant should have at least one preliminary meeting with an individual.

Another potential problem is that one member of the panel may dominate the meeting. This can be avoided by reminding the panel that all members must take part and

EXHIBIT 20

A Structured Interview Guide

STRUCTURED INTERVIEW GUIDE

Name of applicant:_____

Address:_____

_____

Telephone:_____

Position:_____

Interviewed by:_____Date:_____

	Notes and Comments
I. Job Factors–General. (Ask these questions for the applicant's last *three* positions.) 1. On your application you indicated you worked for _____. How long were you employed there? 2. Please describe your responsibilities and duties with this company. 3. What were some of the things you particularly enjoyed on that job? 4. What were some of the things you enjoyed least in that position? 5. Tell me what you consider to be your major accomplishment at that company.	

6. Tell me about some of your set-
   backs and disappointments on that
   job.

7. Tell me about the progress you
   made while with that company.

8. (If progress was significant, ask:)
   To what do you attribute this fine
   progress?
   (If progress was not impressive,
   ask:) Were you satisfied with your
   progress?
   (If not, ask:) How did you attempt to
   overcome this?

9. What was the most valuable experience you obtained in that position?

10. Why did you leave (or why do you
    want to leave) this company?

(Use additional paper if needed for each job covered.)

II. **Education.** (use questions in part A
for applicants who did not attend a
university. Use questions in part B for
those who have had some university
education or who are graduates.)

A. For applicants who did not attend a
university.

1. What was the highest level of
   schooling you completed?

2. Why did you decide not to continue your formal education?

3. How were your overall grades?

**Notes and
Comments**

4. In what extracurricular activities did you participate?

5. Tell me about the class or club offices you held.

6. If you worked, how many hours a week? What kind of jobs?

7. What steps have you taken to acquire additional education since leaving high school?

8. What training did you have in high school (or special schools) that helped your career?

9. What was the first significant job you held after leaving high school?

10. How did this lead to your present career?

B. For university graduates and those who have had some university education.

1. I see that you attended _____ University. Why did you select that school?

2. What was your major? What determined this choice?

3. What were your overall university grades? How did they compare with your high school grades?

4. What courses did you start in the university and later drop? Why?

5. In what types of extracurricular activities did you participate in the university? In high school? Offices held?

6. How did you finance your university education?

7. If you worked in high school or the university, how many hours per week? Summers? What type jobs?

8. What were your vocational plans when you were in the university?

9. If they are different now, when did you change your thinking? Why?

10. What additional education have you had since you graduated from the university?

11. How do you think your university education contributed to your career?

12. (If a university education was not completed.) When did you leave the university? Why? Have you ever planned to complete your degree? What steps have you taken? What results?

13. What was the first significant job you had after leaving (graduating from) the university?

14. How did this lead to your current career?

III. Technical or Special Factors.

Questions related to specialized skills, training and experience should be developed for each type of work for which applicants are being interviewed.

IV. Intangible Factors.

A. GOALS AND MOTIVATION

1. Tell me about your career goals, short-term and long-term.

2. How do you expect to reach these goals?

3. In what way would a job with our company meet your career objectives?

4. What are your criteria for your own success?

5. What factors in the past have contributed most to your own growth?

6. What factors do you believe may have handicapped you from moving ahead more rapidly?

7. When did you decide to go into this career area? What influenced you to make this decision?

8. If you had to do it all over again, what changes would you make in your life and career?

9. What aspects of a job are important to you?

10. What are your present earnings expectations? How did you arrive at this figure?

11. What do you seek in this job that you are not getting in your present job?

B. JOB PERFORMANCE AND ATTITUDES

12. How would you describe the most effective superior you have had? What were his or her strengths? Limitations? Describe your least effective supervisor.

13. In the past, on what have superiors complimented you? For what have they criticized you?

14. Tell me about some of the significant problems you encountered on your jobs. How did you approach them?

15. If you join our company, where do you think you can make the best contribution?

16. In what areas could we help you develop yourself?

General Comments and Recommendations:

that no one member should play a more important role than the others—which may not always be possible.

A variation of the panel interview is two consecutive interviews, with two people conducting each one. This combines the time-saving advantage of the panel interview with the less-formal and less-intimidating setting of a smaller meeting.

THE STRUCTURED INTERVIEW

Some interviewers prefer to use a structured guide to insure that they cover every important area and obtain all key information. The structured interview guide shown in Exhibit 20 contains standard questions for all applicants and places to jot down answers and notes.

Part I of the structured interview guide covers general job factors. A series of questions seeks data on each of the applicant's past three jobs. Only the key information needed to help you remember the applicant should be written down.

Part II covers educational background. One section can be used for applicants who have not had a university education; the other for those who have. This part is particularly valuable for interviewing applicants who have completed their formal education less than five years ago.

Part III is aimed at evaluating technical or specialized expertise. You must compile questions according to your own job requirements. Part IV covers intangibles such as goals and attitudes. After the interview, additional comments can be indicated on the bottom of the page.

One advantage of the guide is that you can easily compare candidates since all have been asked the same basic questions. However, the guide does deprive the interview of spontaneity and tends to make all interviews similar.

Sometimes interviewers may become so anxious to ask the next question on the form that they do not follow through on answers to a previous question—and thereby fail to get valuable information.

How to Use the Form

Effective use demands flexibility. The form is a guide, not an authoritative document. It is not necessary to ask every question of every applicant. If the response to one question is not clear or leads to a question not included in the guide, you should digress. If a question is unnecessary it can—and should—be omitted.

SELECTING THE BEST APPROACH

The best interviewing approach depends on the size of the company, the organizational structure, and the importance of the job for which the interview is being held.

A small company may not need nor have the facilities for multiple interviews. One screening interview by a lower-level manager followed by an interview conducted by the manager to whom the applicant will report is sufficient. If an additional opinion is desired, an interview with another member of management can usually be arranged.

In a medium-sized company with several department heads and other persons in management positions, serial interviews are particularly effective. Panel interviews may also be effective. However, if panel interviews are used, each participant should be instructed in the techniques to be used. Whatever system is used, each interviewer should be trained in interviewing and instructed in how to use the interview summary or screening interview summary forms.

Here is another chance for you to exhibit your skills. You have the necessary expertise to advise other managers on the best interviewing techniques. You know how to develop and use summary forms and how to conduct various types of interviews. Dispense that knowledge. And garner the recognition.

29

THE JOB OFFER
INTERVIEW

After a decision has been reached on the person to be hired, the selected applicant is invited back for a job-offer interview. At this meeting all of the details of the offer should be explained and any questions that the applicant may have about the offer answered.

There should be clear understandings about:

- Compensation and benefits

- Conditions of the offer

- Relocation requirements (if applicable)

- Travel requirements

- Starting date

- Deadline on acceptance of offer

- Special job requirements

Compensation and benefits.   The salary is restated in the job-offer interview so that there is no misunderstanding. If benefits are explained in a company pamphlet, giving it to the selected candidate is sufficient. Special benefits that apply only to the applicant can be explained orally.

Conditions of the offer.   Often a job offer is made subject to certain conditions such as passing a physical examination; receipt by the company of references, of proof of citizenship, or of proof that the applicant has the necessary licenses, academic degree, or other requirements for the job. Any such conditions should be explained with the understanding that the job offer will be withdrawn if they are not met.

Relocation requirements.   If the job involved immediate relocation, the company and applicant should agree when the move will take place. Who pays and how the cost of relocating will be borne should also be discussed. If relocation may be required in the future, this fact should also be discussed. If the applicant has strong reservations about moving, the company must weigh the value of potential sevices against the need to have the relocation.

Travel requirements.   The amount of travel, if any, that the job entails should be completely spelled out. How travel expenses will be handled should also be discussed and made clear.

Starting date.   Currently employed applicants will most likely have to give notice to their employers that they are leaving. A definite starting date must be established during the job-offer interview.

Deadline on acceptance. Some applicants may not be ready to accept an offer. They may have reservations about the job or offers from other companies that they want to consider. Therefore, an offer should have a reasonable deadline set for a decision by the applicant.

Special job requirements. Any aspects of the job that may affect the applicant outside normal office work and hours are discussed in detail during the job-offer interview.

Should the Offer be Oral or Written?

Most companies make the job offers orally. Some confirm them in writing. Others make the initial offer in a letter. Many are formal in hiring new people for management, technical, or other senior positions. A sample job-offer letter is shown in Exhibit 21. In this instance, an oral offer was made and the letter confirms it.

Countering the Counteroffer

After an applicant has accepted an offer, he or she may receive a counteroffer from their present employer. To prevent a protracted struggle or reversal of a previous acceptance you should assume that *every* currently employed applicant will be tendered a counteroffer. One strategy is to prepare the applicant to reject the counteroffer at the same time you make your own offer.

Here are some good defensive tactics for undermining a future counteroffer:

EXHIBIT 21

Sample Job-Offer Letter

S & L T O O L C O M P A N Y
6 Townsend Avenue
Park Grove, New York 10003

June 1, 1984

Mr. Louis B. Higgins
999 Main Street
Garden City, N.Y. 11530

Dear Mr. Higgins:

This will confirm the job offer we made when you were
in our office yesterday. We are pleased to offer you the
position of Office Manager in our headquarters office.
The salary will be $24,000 per year, payable semi-
monthly. A pamphlet outlining our benefits package is
enclosed. In addition we will pay your relocation expenses to our city except for any lease commitments
you may now have on your apartment. This offer is
subject to your passing our company physical examination.

We understand that you will let us know your decision
no later than two weeks from this date and will be
able to start work two weeks after that.

We look forward to having you join our organization
and are confident that this will result in a mutually
advantageous relationship.

Sincerely,

Alfred Jones
Vice President—Administration

AJ:mdl

Enc.

—"From what you've said, I think your firm may make
a counteroffer. If it does, you might want to consider
it carefully. A counteroffer is made for the company's
benefit—not yours. If your former employer thought
enough of you to give you a higher salary, he would
have done so before you gave notice. If you accept
that counteroffer, he may think of you as a manip-
ulator who used a job offer to obtain more money."

—"In the future, you may be looked upon as disloyal—someone who is out for individual gain at the expense of the company."

—"The company will probably start training somebody to learn your job. It won't want to be surprised again if you decide to repeat this—and it may replace you at its convenience."

—"Next time a salary increment is due, you may find that you have been bypassed."

Making these arguments *before* the applicant gives notice reduces the chances of a counteroffer being accepted.

Employment Contracts

Is a contract desirable? The answer to this is governed chiefly by industry and company custom. Most companies do not give a new employee a contract. There are a few exceptions to this. Senior executives sometimes ask for and are granted contracts on an individual basis. Salespeople who have a following among their customers are often given contracts. Key employees with access to company secrets may be asked to sign secrecy agreements that bind them not to divulge secrets.

Another type of contract is used by some employers to restrict employees from working for competitors for a specified period of time after they leave the employ of the company. Other restrictive clauses prohibit dissemination of technical information without approval from a higher-ranking officer of the company. Technical people often sign contracts releasing any patent rights they may have on products designed for the company.

EXHIBIT 22

Sample Rejection Letter

S & L T O O L C O M P A N Y
6 Townsend Avenue
Park Grove, New York 10003

June 1, 1984

Mr. Thomas F. Burns
605 Broadway
New York, N.Y. 10017

Dear Mr. Burns:

It was not an easy decision for us but, after
careful deliberation, we felt that another
candidate for the office manager's position
was closer to our job specification.

This is in no way a reflection on the quality
of your background, or your character.
All of the people in our company who
interviewed you liked you. Your experience is certainly excellent.

We wish you the best of luck in your career. With the strengths you have, you are sure to be an asset to some company. We sincerely regret it couldn't be ours.

Sincerely,

Alfred Jones
Vice President—Administration

AJ:mdl

Contacting Rejected Applicants

Applicants not hired are notified of their rejections. Although it is not necessary to tell an applicant the specific reason for the rejection, it is discourteous and unbusinesslike to ignore them.

The most diplomatic way is to tell all applicants, in advance, that there are several candidates for the job and that you intend to select the one closest to your requirements. Then, when the applicant is rejected, all you have to say is that one of the other applicants was more qualified for the job.

Those applicants who have been under serious consideration and have had several interviews, but have not been offered a position, should be sent friendly, personal letters.

A sample rejection letter is shown in Exhibit 22.

APPENDICES

These four appendices were designed for you to use to further hone your employee selection skills. They are not merely for reference. Look them over. Make copies and pass them around. You'll not only improve your techniques, but attain a higher profile among key audiences in your firm.

Appendix A shows you the type of information available on testing today. It will give you a good idea of what's on the market, and what's not.

Appendix B tells you where to go to obtain further information on those tests.

Appendix C is an interviewer self-evaluation checklist. Use it to judge how well you've incorporated the techniques in this book into your personal interviewing style. Give it to your subordinates to rate their efforts.

Appendix D is a good background handout for providing a brief overview of employee interviewing. It will be helpful to anyone involved in the interviewing process.

SELECTED TESTS

One of the largest reference libraries of tests and measurement devices is Test Collections, Educational Testing Service, Princeton, New Jersey 08541. The variety of services offered by Test Collections is described in Chapter 20.

To give you an idea of the extensive nature of the tests available today for measuring job/intelligence/personal attributes that contribute to the selection process, this Appendix lists an abbreviated version of some of the more common bibliographies.

The first section is a complete listing from Test Collections for Measures of Clerical Aptitude and Achievement. It is representative of such listings.

The tests are listed alphabetically and contain title, publisher or distribution organization, and a brief description of what is contained in the test or evaluated by it.

Specific information on each test and/or specimen sets must be obtained directly from the publisher/distributor. See Appendix B for names and addresses.

The second section of this Appendix is designed to familiarize you with some of the other common business areas in which extensive lists of tests are available. Included are the first pages from tests such as:

- Group-administered intelligence
- Individually-administered intelligence
- Engineering aptitude and achievement
- Occupational knowledge tests: skilled trades
- Mechanical aptitude
- Data processing aptitude
- Manual dexterity
- Vocational interest
- General measures of personality.

SECTION I

MEASURES OF
CLERICAL APTITUDE
AND ACHIEVEMENT

A.C.E.R. Short Clerical Test; c1953–56; Ages: 13 and over; Australian Council for Educational Research.
Designed for use in selecting clerical workers. Tests ability to perceive, remember, and check written or printed matter; also measures simple arithmetic skills.

ACT Career Planning Program: Revised Edition, Form H; c1976; Ages: 16 and over; American College Testing Program.
A guidance-oriented system designed to help students identify and explore personally relevant occupational and educational programs. The instrument is in four parts; Vocational Interest Profile (Business Contact, Business Detail, Trades, Technology, Science, Health, Creative Arts, Social Service); Experience Scales (same subscales as the VIP except for Health); Ability Measures (Mechanical Reasoning, Numerical Skills, Space Relations, Reading Skills, Language Usage, Clerical Skills); and Student Information Section (Educational and

Vocational Plans, Biographical Information, Educational Needs, Local Items).

Application for Position (Clerical); c1965; Ages: Adults; Stevens, Thurow, and Associates, Inc.

A screening form for determining the range of skills and general fitness of applicants for clerical positions.

Aptitude Tests for Occupations by Wesley S. Roeder; c1951; Grades: 9–16 and adults; Bobbs-Merrill Company, Inc.

Designed to aid in vocational counseling through the assessment of occupation-related aptitudes and potentialities. The battery includes tests for: Personal-Social Aptitude, Mechanical Aptitude, General Sales Aptitude, Clerical Routine Aptitude, Computational Aptitude, and Scientific Aptitude.

Armed Services Vocational Aptitude Battery; c1967–Present; Grades: 9–12 and adults; Armed Forces Vocational Testing Group.

A group of 9 tests designed to assess aptitude in 5 vocational-technical areas: General/Technical, Motor Mechanics, General Mechanics, Clerical/Administrative, and Electronics. The tests include: Coding Speed, Word Knowledge, Arithmetic Reasoning, Tool Knowledge, Space Perception, Mechanical Comprehension, Shop Information, Automotive Information, and Electronics Information.

Certified Professional Secretary Examination; 1965; Ages: Adults; Institute for Certifying Secretaries.

Examinations are in: Behavioral Science in Business, Business Law, Economics and Management, Accounting, Communications and Decision-Making, and Office Procedures and Administration.

Classifying Test; c1950–63; Ages: Adults; Richardson, Bellows, Henry, and Company, Inc.

A clerical aptitude test. Measures both speed and accuracy in classifying material.

Clerical Aptitude Test by A. Kobal, J.W. Wrightstone, K.R. Kunze, Major A.J. MacElroy; c1943–62; Grades: 7 and over; Psychometric Affiliates.

Covers: Business practice; number checking; date, name and address checking.

Clerical Skills Series; c1966; Ages: Adults; Martin M. Bruce, Publishers.

Designed to measure proficiency in paperwork tasks typical of activities in common clerical occupations. Subtests include: alphabetizing-filing, arithmetic, clerical speed and accuracy, coding, eye-hand accuracy, grammar and punctuation, spelling, spelling-vocabulary, vocabulary and word fluency.

Clerical Tests, Series N; c1951–59; Ages: Adults; Stevens, Thurow and Associates.

Designed for personnel directors and office and factory executives for improved selection of clerical personnel.

Clerical Tests, Series V; c1951–59; Ages: Adults; Stevens, Thurow, and Associates.

Designed for personnel directors and office and factory executives for improved selection of clerical personnel.

Clerical Worker Examination; c1962–63; Ages: Adults; McCann Associates.

Subscores: Speed and Accuracy in Routine Work, Verbal Learning Ability, Quantitative Learning Ability, Total Learning Ability.

Curtis Verbal-Clerical Skills Tests by James W. Curtis; c1963–65; Ages: Adults; Psychometric Affiliates.

Devised to provide estimates of individual competence in four basic areas of verbal skill usually identified with office and clerical work, as well as with potential for training at the advanced or college level. Includes capacity test, computation test, checking test, and comprehension test.

Detroit Clerical Aptitudes Examination by Harry J. Baker, Paul H. Voelker; c1967; Grades: 7-12; Bobbs-Merrill Company, Inc. Designed to discover and select pupils who have abilities suitable for commercial courses in high school. Subtests are: Motor (Circles, Classification), Visual Imagery, (Likeness and Differences, Disarranged Pictures), Trade Information, Educational (Handwriting, Arithmetic, Alphabetizing).

Detroit General Aptitudes Examination, Form A by Harry J. Baker, Paul H. Voelker, Alex C. Crockett; c1938-1954; Grades: 6-12; Bobbs-Merrill Company, Inc.

Test is designed specifically for use in the junior and senior high schools. Measures three kinds of aptitudes: intelligence, mechanical, and clerical. Test may be used to classify the interests of pupils and for individual counseling and guidance.

Differential Aptitude Tests: Forms L and M by George K. Bennett, Harold G. Seashore, Alexander G. Wesman; c1947-67; Grades: 8-12 and adults; The Psychological Corporation.

An integrated battery of aptitude tests designed for educational and vocational guidance. Provides a profile of relative strengths and weaknesses in eight abilities. Verbal Reasoning, Numerical Ability, Abstract Reasoning, Space Relations, Mechanical Reasoning, Clerical Speed and Accuracy, Spelling, and Language Usage.

Differential Aptitude Tests: Forms S and T by George K. Bennett, Harold G. Seashore, Alexander G. Wesman; c1947-73; Grades: 8-12 and adults; The Psychological Corporation.

Provides a profile of students' strengths and weaknesses in eight abilities: Verbal Reasoning, Numerical Ability, Abstract Reasoning, Space Relations, Mechanical Reasoning, Clerical Speed and Accuracy, Spelling, and Language Usage.

ETSA Test 3-A: General Clerical Ability Test by S. Trevor Hadley, George A.W. Stouffer; c1957-60; Ages: Adults; Employers' Tests and Services Associates.

Designed to measure the general skills required of clerks in routine office work. Subscores are: Alphabetizing, Matching

Numbers, Name Checking, Spelling, Office Vocabulary, and Mailing.

ETSA Test 4-A: Stenographic Skills Test by S. Trevor Hadley, George A.W. Stouffer; c1957–60; Ages: Adults; Employers' Tests and Services Associates.

Designed to measure typing and/or shorthand and the general skills required of secretaries and stenographers. Subscores are: Spelling, Filing, Grammar, General Information.

Employee Aptitude Survey – Prueba 2, Hablidad Numerica by Floyd L. Ruch, Neil D. Warren, Glen Grimsley, James S. Ford; c1969; Ages: Adults; Educational and Industrial Testing Service.

This Spanish edition of EAS – Test 2, Numerical Ability measures the ability to work easily with numbers and perform simple arithmetic. Subtests include: integers, decimals, and common fractions.

Employee Aptitude Survey – Prueba 4, Rapidez y Precision Visual by Floyd L. Ruch, Neil D. Warren, Glen Grimsley, James S. Ford; c1969; Ages: Adults; Educational and Industrial Testing Service.

This Spanish edition of EAS – Test 4, Visual Speed and Accuracy measures the ability to perceive small detail rapidly and accurately within a mass of material.

Employee Aptitude Survey – Test 2, Numerical Ability by G. Grimsley, F.L. Ruch, N.D. Warren; c1952–63; Ages: Adults; Psychological Services, Inc.

Measures the ability to work easily with numbers, to do simple arithmetic fast and accurately. Subtests include integers, decimals and common fractions.

Employee Aptitude Survey – Test 4, Visual Speed and Accuracy by G. Grimsley, F.L. Ruch, N.D. Warren; c1952–63; Ages: Adults; Psychological Services, Inc.

A measure of the ability to see small details quickly and accurately, as in visual inspection and clerical work.

Flanagan Aptitude Classification Tests: 19-Test Edition by John C. Flanagan; Science Research Associates, Inc.

Measures an individual's aptitude for 19 skills essential to success in 37 broad occupational areas. The skills are: Inspection, Mechanics, Tables, Reasoning, Vocabulary, Assembly, Judgment and Comprehension, Components, Planning, Arithmetic, Ingenuity, Scales, Expression, Precision, Alertness, Coordination, Patterns, Coding, Memory.

Flanagan Industrial Tests: Form A by John C. Flanagan; c1960–65; Ages: Adults; Science Research Associates, Inc.

An adaptation of the Flanagan Aptitude Classification Tests for use in business and industry. Consists of 18 separate tests: Arithmetic, Assembly, Components, Coordination, Electronics, Expression, Ingenuity, Inspection, Judgment and Comprehension, Mathematics and Reasoning, Mechanics, Memory, Patterns, Planning, Precision, Scales, Tables, and Vocabulary.

General Aptitude Test Battery (GATB); c1946–68; Grades: 9–16 and adults; any State Employment Service Office.

A multiple-aptitude test battery. Nine aptitudes are measured: Intelligence, Verbal Aptitude, Numerical Aptitude, Spatial Aptitude, Form Perception, Clerical Perception, Motor Coordination, Finger Dexterity, and Manual Dexterity.

General Clerical Test; c1944–72; Grades 9–12 and over; The Psychological Corporation.

Designed to assess abilities which are important in all types of clerical office work. Provides for: Clerical Speed and Accuracy, Numerical Ability, and Verbal Facility.

Guilford-Zimmerman Aptitude Survey by J.P. Guilford, Wayne S. Zimmerman; 1947–65; Grades: 9–16 and adults; Sheridan Psychological Services.

Subtests: Verbal Comprehension, General Reasoning, Numerical Operations, Perceptual Speed, Spatial Orientation, Spatial Visualization. Designed to measure abstract intelligence, clerical aptitudes and mechanical aptitudes.

Hiett Diamond Jubilee Series Shorthand Test by Victor C. Hiett; c1963; Grades: 9–16; Bureau of Educational Measurements.
Designed to assess shorthand ability.

Hiett Simplified Shorthand Test by V.C. Hiett, H.E. Schrammel; c1951; Grades: 9–16; Bureau of Educational Measurements.
Test includes reading and writing of shorthand characters, dictation and interpretation of notes.

Instructional Objectives Exchange: Objective Collection in Business Education – Secretarial Skills, Grades 10–12; Not dated (circa 1970); Grades: 10–12; The Instructional Objectives Exchange.
Consists of a number of instructional objectives based upon curricular materials and a pool of items to assess the attainment of the objective. Covers typing, shorthand, office machines, filing, telephone answering and processing, basic forms of business English, and the fundamentals of office behavior and appearance.

International Primary Factors Test Battery by Wolfgang O. Horn; c1973; Grades: 5–12 and adults; International Tests, Incorporated.
A group-administered aptitude battery. Subtests are: Vocabulary (Verbal Comprehension), Word Fluency, Memory for Words, Memory for Numbers, Memory for Designs, Mazes (Practical Efficiency, Porteus), Reasoning with Designs, Reasoning with Letters and Numbers, Hidden Designs (Closure 2), Unfolding Solids (Space 2), Mutilated Pictures (Closure 3), Mutilated Words (Closure 1), Spelling, Addition (Number), Comparison of Words (Perceptual Speed), and Comparison of Numbers (Perceptual Speed).

Job – Tests Program by J.E. King, H.B. Osborn, Jr., R.B. Cattell, A.K. Schuettler; c1947–60; Ages: Adults; Industrial Psychology, Inc.
A battery of aptitude tests, personality tests, and biographical forms used in various combinations to assess for jobs in

business and industry. Includes a Factored Aptitude Series (Office Terms, Sales Terms, Factory Terms, Tools, Numbers, Perception, Judgment, Precision, Fluency, Memory, Parts, Blocks, Dimension, Dexterity, Motor), an Employee Attitude Series (Contact Personality Factor, Neurotic Personality Factor, 16 Personality Factor), and an Application Interview Series (Clerical, Mechanical, Sales, Technical, Supervisor).

Measurement of Skills by Walter V. Clarke, et al; c1956–66; Ages: Adults; Walter V. Clarke Associates, Inc.

Designed as aids in the proper selection, classification and assignment of business and industrial employees at all levels of the occupational hierarchy. Measures skills with vocabulary, numbers, shapes, speed and accuracy, orientation...thinking, memory, fingers and typing.

Micro-Tower System of Vocational Evaluation; c1977; Ages: Adolescent – Adult; ICD Rehabilitation and Research Center.

Aptitudes necessary for a variety of unskilled and semiskilled occupations are assessed by a battery of specific work samples. Strengths and weaknesses are identified in the following areas: motor spatial, clerical perception, verbal and numerical norms available for a variety of disadvantaged groups.

Minnesota Clerical Test by Dorothy M. Andre, Donald G. Paterson, Howard P. Longstaff; c1933–59; Grades: 7–12 and adults; The Psychological Corporation.

Measures aptitude for certain aspects of clerical work; often supplemented with a test of general mental ability. The test is used for selection of clerks, inspectors, office workers, and others whose jobs depend on speedy perception and rapid handling of numbers, letters, or symbols.

New York State Regents High School Examinations Combination Shorthand, Typewriting and Transcription; 1865–Present; Grades: 9–12; The University of the State of New York Press.

New York State Regents High School Examinations Shorthand II and Transcription; 1865–Present; Grades: 9–12; University of the State of New York Press.

New York State Regents High School Examinations Typewriting I; 1865–Present; Grades: 9–12; University of the State of New York Press.

Number Checking Test, Form I; c1957; Ages: Adults; Richardson, Bellows, Henry, and Company, Inc.
Used in situations where proofreading, auditing, or other clerical checking is involved.

Office Skills Achievement Test by Karl L. Mellenbruch; c1962; Grades: 9–12 and adults; Psychometric Affiliates.
Subscores are: Business Letter, Grammar, Checking, Filing, Arithmetic, Written Directions.

Office Skills Tests by Bruce A. Campbell, Joan M. Costello, LaVonne Macaitis, Barbara Steiger; c1977; Ages: Adults; Science Research Associates, Inc.
Subtests: Checking, Coding, Filing, Forms, Completion, Grammar, Numerical Skills, Oral Directions, Punctuation, Reading Comprehension, Spelling, Typing, Vocabulary.

Office Worker Test; c1956–72; Ages: Adults; International Personnel Management Association.
Subscores are: Checking, Filing, Vocabulary, Computation, Spelling, Punctuation, Reasoning, Reading, English Usage, Office Information.

Purdue Clerical Adaptability Test by C.H. Lawshe, Joseph Tiffin, Herbert Moore; c1949–56; Ages: Adults; University Book Store.
Aids in the selection of clerical and office personnel.

RBH Coding Test, Form I; c1948–63; Ages: Adults; Richardson, Bellows, Henry and Company, Inc.
Measures ability to see details quickly and to recognize likeness and differences.

RBH Individual Background Survey, Form T; c1952–63; Ages: Adults; Richardson, Bellows, Henry and Company, Inc.

Designed to provide information concerning a person's background and personal history. Four keys have been developed: female clerical, male clerical, male industrial, and male sales and professional.

RBH Industrial Questionnaire; c1957; Ages: Adults; Richardson, Bellows, Henry, and Company, Inc.

Test can be administered to blue-collar workers, unskilled labor and routine factory workers, operatives and craftsmen, vehicle operators, plant clerks, and warehousemen. Includes items on reading comprehension, arithmetic reasoning, and chemical comprehension.

RBH Language Skills and Dictation Test: Form I; c1957; Ages: Adults; Richardson, Bellows, Henry and Company, Inc.

Designed to test one's ability to produce accurate, finished copy from material other than one's own shorthand notes and one's ability to take dictation.

Reicherter-Sanders Typewriting I and II Test by Richard F. Reicherter, M.W. Sanders; c1964; Grades: 9–12; Bureau of Educational Measurements.

Test measures speed and accuracy.

SRA Clerical Aptitudes; c1947–50; Grades: 9–12 and adults; Science Research Associates, Inc.

Designed to estimate an individual's ability to learn and perform clerical tasks. The test yields scores for office vocabulary, office arithmetic, and office checking.

SRA Typing 5 by Steven J. Stanard, LaVonne Macaitis; c1975; Ages: Adults; Science Research Associates, Inc.

These three five-minute typing tests are designed to measure speed and accuracy in various kinds of typing assignments. Three forms are available: Typing Speed, Business Letter, and Numerical.

SRA Typing Skills Test by Marion W. Richardson, Ruth A. Pederson; c1947–65; Ages: Adults; Science Research Associates, Inc.

Measure of typing ability. Yields an International Speed Score and an Accuracy Ratio.

Seashore-Bennett Stenographic Proficiency Test by George K. Bennett; c1946–56; Ages: Adults; The Psychological Corporation.

Subscores: Typing: Neatness and Cleanliness, Arrangement, Quality of Stroke, Errors; English: Errors; Shorthand: Errors.

Selection Tests for Office Personnel by Walter A. Eggert, Albert H. Malo; c1962–64; Ages: Adults; Kemper Insurance.

A series of ten tests designed to measure the most commonly used abilities and traits in an insurance office. The tests are: Language Skills, Data Perception, Arithmetic, Coding, Rating, Personality, Filing, Stenography, Spelling, and Typing. The employer administers only those tests which measure the skills needed for a specific job.

Short Employment Tests by George K. Bennett, Marjorie Gelink; c1951–72; Ages: Adults; The Psychological Corporation.

A battery of aptitude tests designed to assess clerical applicants and personnel. The tests include: Verbal, Numerical and Clerical Aptitude.

Short Occupational Knowledge Test for Office Machine Operators by Bruce A. Campbell, Suellen O. Johnson; c1970; Ages: Adults; Science Research Associates, Inc.

Designed for use in hiring, placement, or reassignment. Three scores are provided: Pass, Fail, or Unclassifiable.

Short Occupational Knowledge Test for Secretaries by Bruce A. Campbell, Suellen O. Johnson; c1969; Ages: Adults; Science Research Associates, Inc.

Designed to determine how familiar an applicant or employee is with the content and concepts of the occupational areas.

Short Tests of Clerical Ability by Jean Maier Palormo; c1959–60; Ages: Adults; Science Research Associates, Inc.

Designed to measure an aptitude or ability important to the successful performance of tasks which are common parts of various office jobs. Subtests include: business vocabulary, arithmetic, checking, filing, directions–oral and written, coding and language.

Stevens, Thurow and Associates Clerical Tests: Inventory J, Arithmetical Reasoning; c1951–66; Ages: Adults; Stevens, Thurow and Associates, Inc.

Test can be used to aid in the selection of certain positions where specific skills and abilities are required.

Stevens, Thurow and Associates Clerical Tests: Inventory K, Arithmetical Proficiency; c1951–66; Ages: Adults; Stevens, Thurow and Associates, Inc.

Test can be used to aid in the selection of certain positions where specific skills and abilities are required.

Stevens, Thurow and Associates Clerical Tests: Inventory M – Interpretation of Tabulated Material; c1951; Ages: Adults; Stevens, Thurow and Associates, Inc.

Stevens, Thurow and Associates Clerical Tests: Inventory R – Interpretation of Tabulated Material; c1951; Ages: Adults; Stevens, Thurow and Associates, Inc.

Stevens, Thurow and Associates Clerical Tests: Inventory S – Alphabetical Filing; c1951; Ages: Adults; Stevens, Thurow and Associates, Inc.

Stevens, Thurow and Associates Clerical Tests: Inventory Y – Grammar; c1951; Ages: Adults; Stevens, Thurow and Associates.

Designed to measure the clerical skills of grammar or diction, and alphabetical filing.

Steward Basic Factors Inventory: 1960 Edition by Verne Steward; c1960; Ages: Adults; Steward-Mortensen and Associates.
Designed for use with sales and office personnel. The subtests are: Business Knowledge (Vocabulary, Arithmetic), Dominance and Personal Adjustment, and Occupational Interests (clerical, artistic, supervisory, accounting, writing, selling, mechanics).

Symbol Identities by Ralph Hoepfner, J.P. Guilford; Not dated; Grades: 9–16 and adults; Sheridan Psychological Services, Inc.
A measure of the factor evaluation of symbolic units. The examinee is presented with pairs of sets of symbols (words, names, numbers) and is required to determine whether the pair members are exactly alike or are different. Norms are available for grade 10. Included in the battery, Southern California Tests of Intellectual Abilities.

Test of Typing Speed; c1958–63; Ages: Adults; Richardson, Bellows, Henry, and Company, Inc.
A 5-minute test of speed of typing.

Typing Test for Business by Jerome E. Doopelt, Arthur D. Hartman, Fay B. Krawchick; c1967; Ages: Adults; The Psychological Corporation.
Designed to assess competence within the various areas of typing. Areas include practice copy, straight copy, letters, revised manuscript, numbers and tables.

USES Clerical Skills Tests; c1968; Ages: Adults; United States Employment Service.
This test is for use only by state employment services, federal and state agencies. Subtests are: Typing, Dictation, Spelling, Statistical Typing, Medical Spelling, and Legal Spelling.

United States Training and Employment Service Nonreading Aptitude Test Battery: 1969 Edition; 1969–1970; Grades: 9–12 and adults; United States Training and Employment Service.

Tests: Picture Word Matching, Coin Matching, Matrices, Tool Matching, Three Dimensional Space, Form Matching, Coin Series, Name Comparison, Mark Making, Place, Form, Assemble, Disassemble, Oral Vocabulary. Measures the same nine aptitudes as the General Aptitude Test Battery: Intelligence, Verbal Aptitude, Numerical Aptitude, Spatial Aptitude, Form Perception, Clerical Perception, Motor Coordination, Finger Dexterity, and Manual Dexterity. The NATB was designed specifically for the disadvantaged. The test is not available on an open-sales basis. For information, contact your State Employment Service.

Vocabulary Test, Form I; c1948–63; Ages: Adults; Richardson, Bellows, Henry and Company, Inc.

Measures understanding of the meanings of words and the relationships between them.

SECTION II

GROUP-ADMINISTERED MEASURES OF INTELLIGENCE

Academic Aptitude Test—Non-Verbal Intelligence: Psychometric Affiliates.

The test consists of three parts: spatial relations, comprehension of physical relations, and graphic relations.

Academic Aptitude Test—Verbal Intelligence: Psychometric Affiliates.

Designed to judge the abilities of an applicant for employment in a position which requires independent judgment or mental alertness. Factors include: general information, mental alertness, and comprehension of relations.

Altus Information Inventory: Educational Testing Service.
Designed to provide a measure of general intelligence for
screening purposes.

Cattell Culture Fair Intelligence Test: Bobbs-Merrill Company,
Inc.
The scale is in two parts, each of which consists of the same
four sub-tests: series, classifications, matrices, conditions.
Scale 2 is for average adults and Scale 3 for superior adults.

Escala de Inteligencia Wechsler para Adultos: The Psychological Corporation.
Spanish adaptation of the Wechsler Adult Intelligence Scale.
Yields scores in two areas: verbal (information, comprehension, arithmetic, similarities, digit span, vocabulary) and performance (digit symbol, picture completion, block design,
picture arrangement, object assembly).

IPAT Culture Fair Intelligence Test: Institute for Personality
and Ability Testing.
A Spanish edition of the scale is available. Subtests are:
series, classifications, matrices, conditions. Scale 2 is for
average adults and Scale 3 for superior adults.

Leiter Adult Intelligence Scale: Stoelting Company.
Designed to measure general intelligence in adults.

Leiter International Performance Scale: Stoelting Company.
A measure of general intelligence. Subtests include: matching
colors, block design, matching pictures, matching circles and
squares, four forms, picture completion, number discrimination, form and color, eight forms; counts four, form, color,
number, genus, two color circles, clothing, analagous progression, pattern completion test, matching on a basis of use,
reconstruction, circle series, circumference series, recognition of age differences, matching shades of gray, form discrimination, judging mass, series of radii, dot estimation,
analagous designs, line completion, footprints recognition

test, concealed cubes, similarities, two things, recognition of facial expressions, classification of animals, memory for a series, form completion test, code for a number series, reversed clocks, and spatial relations test.

INDIVIDUALLY ADMINISTERED MEASURES OF INTELLIGENCE

Arthur Point Scale of Performance Tests, Revised Form II: The Psychological Corporation.
Designed to furnish an I.Q. comparable to that obtained with the Binet scales.

Analysis of Relationships: Consulting Psychologists Press, Inc.
A measure of general intellectual abilities with an emphasis on verbal ability, reasoning, and problem-solving.

Barranquilla Rapid Survey Intelligence Test: The Psychological Corporation.
Provides an index of learning potential by evaluating verbal intelligence and numerical reasoning. Available in Spanish only.

California Short Form Test of Mental Maturity, 1963 S–Form, Level 5: CTB/McGraw-Hill.
Yields scores on logical reasoning, numerical reasoning, verbal concepts and memory.

California Test of Mental Maturity, Long Form, Level 5, 1963: CTB/McGraw-Hill.
Measures various aspects of mental ability. Subtests include: opposites, similarities, analogies, logical reasoning, rights and lefts, manipulation of areas, spatial relationships, numerical values, number problems, numerical reasoning, inferences, verbal comprehension, verbal concepts, immediate and delayed recall, and memory.

Cattell Culture Fair Intelligence Test: Bobbs-Merrill Company, Inc.

Scale is in two parts, each of which consists of the same four subtests; series, classifications, matrices, conditions. Scale 2 is for average adults and Scale 3 is for superior adults.

Chicago Non-Verbal Examination: The Psychological Corporation.

Measures intelligence.

Concept Mastery Test, 1950 Edition: The Psychological Corporation.

A measure of ability to deal with abstract ideas at a high level. Consists of two parts: the identification of synonyms and antonyms, and the completion of analogies.

The D48 Test: Consulting Psychologists Press, Inc.

A nonverbal analogies' measure of general intelligence employing pictures of dominoes. Adapted from the original version of French.

ENGINEERING APTITUDE AND ACHIEVEMENT

Act Career Planning Program: Revised Edition, Form H; c1976; Ages: 16 and over; American College Testing Program.

A guidance-oriented system designed to help students identify and explore personally relevant occupational and educational programs. The instrument is in four parts: vocational interest profile (business contact, business detail, trades, technology, science, health, creative arts, social service); experience scales (same subscales as the VIP except for health); ability measures (mechanical reasoning, numerical skills, space relations, reading skills, language usage, clerical skills); and student information section (educational and vocational plans, biographical information, educational needs, local items).

Algebra Test for Engineering and Science by A.B. Lonski; c1959–61; Grades: 12–13; Psychometric Affiliates.
A test to separate students into homogeneous groups.

Career Ability Placement Survey by Lila Knapp, Robert R. Knapp; c1976; Grades: 7–16; Educational and Industrial Testing Service.
This battery is designed to evaluate abilities pertinent to career development. Tests include: mechanical reasoning, spatial relations, verbal reasoning, numerical ability, language usage, word knowledge, perceptual speed and accuracy, and manual speed and dexterity.

Classifying Test; c1950–63; Ages: Adults; Richardson, Bellows, Henry, and Company, Inc.
Measures both speed and accuracy in classifying material. Norms available for engineering aides.

Garnett College Test in Engineering Science by I. Macfarlane Smith; c1964; Grades: Technical Colleges; NFER-Nelson Publishing Company.
Originally designed for use in experiments on the impact of television broadcasts on students taking the General Course in Engineering Science in Technical Colleges and colleges of further education. Subscores: mechanics, electricity and magnetism.

Graduate Record Examination: Subject Tests – Engineering; 1982; Grades: 16–18; Educational Testing Service.
Designed to measure knowledge and understanding of the engineering field basic to graduate study; designed to be a power rather than speed test. For reasons of fairness, several editions are available each year. Large print answer sheets are available though the test itself is in regular sized print. In developing each new edition, special effort is made to survey the entire academic field and to include material from widely differing curricula. Used for selection of applicants for graduate school, selection of fellowship applicants, guidance and counseling, evaluation of the effectiveness of an

undergraduate or master's program, requirement of conferral of a degree, senior comprehensive examination at the undergraduate level, and comprehensive examination for advancement to a master's or doctoral program. Known as Cooperative Graduate Testing Program until 1940.

OCCUPATIONAL KNOWLEDGE TESTS: SKILLED TRADES

Auto Mechanics Trade Competency Examination: Department of Industrial Education, Eastern Michigan University.
A computer-generated item pool for the assembly of forms on demand – 313 items covering: automotive concepts, testing equipment, engine operation, electrical systems, and chassis.

Bennett Test of Mechanical Comprehension: The Psychological Corporation.
Measures the ability to understand mechanical relationships and physical laws in practical situations. Test is useful in selecting personnel for mechanical work, apprentices, and students for technical and engineering training.

Can You Read A Micrometer?: University Bookstore.
Designed to measure skill in reading a micrometer.

Can You Read A Scale?: University Bookstore.
A test of ability to read a standard scale or rule.

Can You Read A Working Drawing?: University Bookstore.
A test of ability to read a simple working drawing or blueprint.

Carpentry Trade Competency Examination: Eastern Michigan University.
A 218-item pool. Covers: basic fundamentals, hand tools, power tools, fastening, materials, rough carpentry.

Chemical Operators Selection Test: The Dow Chemical Company.

An aptitude test used in the selection of chemical operators personnel. Yields scores on physical principles, tables, graphs, judgment and comprehension, and chemical process from sheet reading.

Circuit Tracing Trainer-Tester for a Black and White Television Receiver: Van Valkenburgh, Nooger and Neville, Inc.

A series of worksheets which describe a problem in the unit. The examinee must investigate the symptoms, isolate the problem, and indicate part replacements or adjustments by erasing ink overprints in designated areas of the worksheet. By numbering each erasure in sequence, the examinee reveals his troubleshooting techniques. The test is scored by judging the adequacy of the problem-solving sequence. Schematic and wiring diagrams, and equipment photographs are supplied.

Drafting Trade Competency Examination: Department of Industrial Education, Eastern Michigan University.

302-items cover: equipment and materials; fundamental operations; dimensioning; shapes, views, and projections; machine drawing; threads and fasteners; architectural drawing; related information; and reproduction drawings.

MEASURES OF MECHANICAL APTITUDE

Aptitude Test for Occupations: CTB/McGraw-Hill.

Designed to aid in vocational counseling through the assessment of occupation-related aptitudes and potentialities. The battery includes tests for: personal-social, mechanical, general sales, clerical routine, computational, and scientific aptitudes.

Bennett Mechanical Comprehension Test: The Psychological Corporation.

This test was designed to measure the ability to perceive and understand the relationship of physical forces and mechanical elements in practical situations.

Bennett Test of Mechanical Comprehension, Form BB-S: The Psychological Corporation.
Spanish edition of the Bennett Test of Mechanical Comprehension.

Differential Aptitude Tests: The Psychological Corporation.
An integrated battery of aptitude tests designed for educational and vocational guidance. Provides a profile of relative strengths and weaknesses in eight abilities: verbal reasoning, numerical ability, abstract reasoning, space relations, mechanical reasoning, clerical speed and accuracy, spelling, and language usage.

ETSA Test 5-A: Mechanical Familiarity: Educators' – Employers' Tests and Service Associates.
Measures the ability to recognize common tools and instruments, which is related to the ability to perform with these devices on the job. Will assist in evaluating those interested in vocational school training along mechanical lines.

Flanagan Aptitude Classification Tests: Science Research Associates, Inc.
Measures an individual's aptitude for 19 skills essential to success in 37 broad occupational areas. The skills are: inspection, mechanics, tables, reasoning, vocabulary, assembly, judgment and comprehension, components, planning, arithmetic, ingenuity, scales, expression, precision, alertness, coordination, patterns, coding, memory.

Guilford-Zimmerman Aptitude Survey—Mechanical Knowledge: Sheridan Psychological Services.
Assesses mechanical knowledge including recognition of tools and their uses, automotive parts and their malfunctions and the meaning of terms related to plumbing, building operations and other trades.

Guilford-Zimmerman Aptitude Survey—Spatial Visualization: Sheridan Psychological Services.

Measures cognition of figural transformations—the ability to manipulate ideas visually.

MEASURES RELATED TO THE DATA PROCESSING FIELD

Aptitude Assessment Battery: Programming by Jack W. Wolfe; c1967, 1969, 1979; Ages: Adults; Wolfe Computer Aptitude Testing, Ltd.

Simulates on-the-job assignments. Covers drawing deductions, understanding complex instructions and specifications, reasoning with symbols, annotating, documenting, desk checking, and debugging. Also in French and Spanish and English for the left-handed.

Berger Systems Analyst General Evaluation: Systems Analysis Test by Frances Berger and Raymond M. Berger; Not dated; Ages: 18–64; Psychometrics, Inc.

Designed as job-related proficiency test for experienced systems analysts, which includes data collection, system acquisition, cost estimation, cost benefit analysis, and system selection and enhancement. Sale of tests is restricted to personnel directors, data processing training directors, and data processing managers. Not sold to individuals.

Berger Systems Analyst General Evaluation: Systems Design and Development Test by Frances Berger and Raymond M. Berger; Not dated; Ages: 18–64; Psychometrics, Inc.

Designed as job-related proficiency test covering areas of analysis of user requirements, evaluation of software, data integrity, reporting requirements, network simulation and interactive systems. Sale of tests is restricted to personnel directors, data processing training directors, and data processing managers. Not sold to individuals.

Berger Systems Analyst General Evaluation: Systems Management Test by Frances Berger and Raymond M. Berger; Not dated; Ages: 18–64; Psychometrics, Inc.

Job-related proficiency test which assesses areas including departmental organization, establishing standards, problems incurred with new procedures, system reviews, feasibility studies, data collection and system conversions. Sale of tests is restricted to personnel directors, data processing training directors, and data processing managers. Not sold to individuals.

Berger Systems Analyst General Evaluation: Systems Testing, Operations, and Maintenance Test by Frances Berger and Raymond M. Berger; Not dated; Ages: 18–64; Psychometrics, Inc.

Job-related proficiency test for experienced personnel. Covers areas including hardware and software knowledge, computer networks, acquisition vs. development, simulation languages, documentation, control procedures, system reviews, limitations of system components, test data generators and operating systems. Sale of tests is restricted to personnel directors, data processing training directors, and data processing managers. Not sold to individuals.

MANUAL DEXTERITY APTITUDE TESTS

APT Manual Dexterity Test: Associated Personnel Technicians, Inc.

Measures the speed with which a person can handle tools.

Career Ability Placement Survey: Educational and Industrial Testing Service.

This battery is designed to evaluate abilities pertinent to career development. Tests include: mechanical reasoning, spatial relations, verbal reasoning, numerical ability, language usage, word knowledge, perceptual speed and accuracy, and manual speed and dexterity.

Crawford Small Parts Dexterity Test: The Psychological Corporation, Inc.

A performance test designed to measure fine eye-hand coordination. Subscores are: tweezer dexterity (pins and collars), and screwdriver dexterity (screws).

Employee Aptitude Survey Test 9 – Manual Speed and Accuracy: Western Psychological Services, Inc.

Measures ability to make quick and accurate movements with the hand.

Employee Aptitude Survey Test 9 – Prueba 9, De Movimientos Manuales: Educational and Industrial Testing Service.

This Spanish edition of EAS – Test 9, Manual Speed and Accuracy measures the ability to make precise, repetitive movements of the fingers rapidly and accurately.

Finger Dexterity Test: Stoelting Company.

Manipulative Aptitude Test: Western Psychological Services.

Measures the ability to make coordinated finger, wrist, hand, and arm movements. Also measures the ability of both hands to work simultaneously or separately.

Hand-Tool Dexterity Test: The Psychological Corporation.

A measure of proficiency in the use of wrenches and screwdrivers.

Minnesota Rate of Manipulation Test: American Guidance Service, Inc.

A measure of manual dexterity consisting of five tests: placing, turning, displacing, one-hand turning and placing, and two-hand turning and placing. A pegboard is required to administer the test. Special directions for administering to the blind are provided.

O'Connor Tweezer Dexterity Test: Stoelting Company.

O'Connor Wiggly Block Test: Lafayette Instrument Company.

Designed to measure imagination, structural and tridimensional visualization.

MEASURES OF VOCATIONAL INTEREST

Ability Self-Rating Inventory: Richard S. Sharf.
Variables assessed: Estimate of ability in 100 occupations which are typical of those which college students might enter. The occupations were selected from the first 100 items of the Strong Vocational Interest Blank, 1965 Edition.

Analysis of Interest: William, Lynde, and Williams.
Designed as a self-study inventory. Yields percentile scores for eight vocational fields: management, accounting, engineering, mechanical, sales, service, teaching, and writing.

California Occupational Preference Survey: Educational and Industrial Testing Service.
Science (professional and skilled), Technical (professional and skilled), Linguistic (professional and skilled), Outdoor, Business (professional and skilled), Clerical, Aesthetic (professional and skilled), Service (professional and skilled).

California Occupational Preference Survey—Spanish Edition: Educational and Industrial Testing Service.
Designed to assist individuals in defining broad areas of occupational interest. Includes thirteen occupational cluster scores obtained in the English (see above), as well as Linguistic (professional and skilled).

Career Assessment Inventory: Interpretive Scoring Systems.
Designed to aid in the career counseling of both students and adults. It is scored in three categories: theme scales (Holland's six vocational types), basic interest scales, and occupational scales.

Career Guidance Inventory in Trades, Services and Technologies: Educational Guidance, Inc.

Provides an indication of relative interest in 25 trade, service, and technical occupations for those individuals who wish to continue their training in a junior college, trade school, or apprentice program.

Comprehensive Occupational Assessment and Training System: PREP, Inc.

Consists of four components: living skills, job matching system, employability attitudes, and work samples. Each component contains three different program levels: assessment and analysis, prescriptions and instruction, and evaluation and placement.

Connolly Occupational Interests: Careers Research and Advisory Centre.

Scientific, social welfare, persuasive, literary, artistic, clerical-computational, and practical.

Crowley Occupational Interests Blank: Careers Research and Advisory Centre.

Yields scores for five interest areas (active-outdoor, office, social, practical, artistic) and five sources of job satisfaction (financial gain, stability-security, companionship, working conditions, interest). It is intended for use with persons of average ability or less.

GENERAL MEASURES OF PERSONALITY

Activity Vector Analysis (AVA): AVA Publications, Inc.

Analysis of personality designed to meet the requirements of business and industry. The four major aspects include: aggressiveness, sociability, emotional stability or emotional control, and social adaptability.

Adjective Check List: Consulting Psychologists Press, Inc.
Subscores: Number of adjectives checked, defensiveness, favorable adjectives checked, unfavorable adjectives checked, self-confidence, self-control, liability, personal adjustment, achievement, dominance, endurance, order, nurturance, affiliation, heterosexuality, exhibition, autonomy, aggression, change, succorance, abasement, deference, counseling readiness.

Behavior Interpretation Inventory: Mortimer H. Appley.
Measures four motives for behavior: escape from present pain or discomfort; avoidance of future pain or discomfort; feeling of belonging; self-realization or self-approval.

Boston University Personality Inventory: Martin A. Jacobs.
Designed to gather information about an individual's personality. Yields scores for four factors; I – passive, compliant, delay, cautious, introversion; II – assertive, defiant, impetuous, danger, extroversion; III – depression, anxiety, hostility, neuroticism; IV – orality.

C.P.F.: Institute for Personality and Ability Testing.
Designed for use in business and industry as a measure of contact vs. noncontact personality (extroversion/introversion) in employees.

California Psychological Inventory: Consulting Psychologists Press, Inc.
Subscores: dominance, capacity for status, sociability, social presence, self-acceptance, sense of well being, responsibility, socialization, self-control, tolerance, good impression, communality, achievement via conformity, achievement via independence, intellectual efficiency, psychological-mindedness, flexibility, femininity.

California Test of Personality: CTB/McGraw-Hill.
Subscores: personal adjustment (self-reliance, sense of personal worth, sense of personal freedom, feeling of belonging,

withdrawing tendencies, nervous symptoms); social adjustment (social standards, social skills, antisocial tendencies, family relations, community relations).

Comrey Personality Scales: Educational and Industrial Testing Service.

A comprehensive multidimensional device for use in assessing eight major personality traits: trust vs. defensiveness, orderliness vs. lack of compulsion, social conformity vs. rebelliousness, activity vs. lack of energy, emotional stability vs. neuroticism, extroversion vs. introversion, masculinity vs. femininity, empathy vs. egocentrism.

MAJOR U.S.
TEST PUBLISHERS

This listing gives you the names and addresses of many of the major business/educational test publishers in the United States. You can write directly to them for further information on the tests they distribute:

Academic Therapy Publications
20 Commercial Boulevard
Novato, CA 94947

The American College Testing
Program (ACT)
P.O. Box 168
Iowa City, IA 52240

Americana Guidance Service,
Inc.
Publishers' Building
Circle Pines, MN 55014

Bureau of Educational
Measurements
Emporia State University
1200 Commercial
Emporia, KS 66801

Bureau of Educational Research
& Service
C-108 Seashore Hall
The University of Iowa
Iowa City, IA 52240

CTB/McGraw Hill
    Western U.S.: (main office)
        Del Monte Research Park
        Monterey, CA 93940
    Eastern U.S.:
        Manchester Road
        Manchester, MO 63011

Charles E. Merrill Publishing Co.
A Bell and Howell Company
1300 Alum Creek Drive
Columbus, OH 43216

Consulting Psychologists Press, Inc.
577 College Avenue
Palo Alto, CA 94306

Educational and Industrial Testing Service
P.O. Box 7234
San Diego, CA 92107

Educational Records Bureau
Box 619
Princeton, NJ 08541

Educational Testing Service
Princeton, NJ 08541
　Western office:
　　1947 Center Street
　　Berkeley, CA 94704
　Midwestern office:
　　One American Plaza,
　　Suite 210
　　Evanston, IL 60201

Guidance Testing Associates
P.O. Box 28096
San Antonio, TX 78228

Institute for Personality and Ability Testing (IPAT)
P.O. Box 188
Champaign, IL 61822

Jastak Associates
1526 Gilpin Avenue
Wilmington, DE 19806

Martin M. Bruce, Ph.D.
Publishers
50 Larchmont Road
Larchmont, NY 10538

Monitor
P.O. Box 2337
Hollywood, CA 90028

NCS Interpretive Scoring Systems
P.O. Box 1416
Minneapolis, MN 55440

National Evaluation Systems
P.O. Box 226
Amherst, MA 01002

PRO-ED
5341 Industrial Oaks Boulevard
Austin, TX 78735

The Psychological Corporation
7500 Old Oak Boulevard
Cleveland, OH 44130

Psychological Test Specialists
Box 9229
Missoula, MT 59807

Psychologists and Educators, Inc.
Suite 212
211 West State Street
Jacksonville, IL 62650

Psychometric Affiliates
Box 3167
Munster, IN 46321

Publishers Test Service
2500 Garden Road
Monterey, CA 93940

Richardson, Bellows, Henry and Company, Inc.
1140 Connecticut Avenue, N.W.
Washington, D.C. 20036

Riverside Publishing Company
8420 Bryn Mawr Avenue
Chicago, IL 60631

Scholastic Testing Service, Inc.
480 Meyer Road
Bensenville, IL 60106

Science Research Associates, Inc.
1555 North Wacker Drive
Chicago, IL 60606

Scott, Foresman and Company
Test Division
1900 East Lake Avenue
Glenview, IL 60025

Sheridan Psychological Services, Inc.
P.O. Box 6101
Orange, CA 92667

Slosson Educational Publications
P.O. Box 280
East Aurora, NY 14052

Stoelting Company
1350 South Kostner
Chicago, IL 60623

Teachers College Press
P.O. Box 1540
Hagerstown, MD 21740

University Bookstore
Purdue University
360 State Street
West Lafayette, IN 47906

Western Psychological Services
12031 Wilshire Boulevard
Los Angeles, CA 90025

INTERVIEWER
SELF-EVALUATION
CHECKLIST

You can improve your interviewing technique by using this checklist after each interview. You may discover that you neglected to use one technique at one meeting, and a different technique at another. Going over the checklist is a good way to remain aware of the multiple elements that go into a productive interview.

<table>
<tr><td></td><td>Yes</td><td>No</td></tr>
</table>

1. **INTRODUCTION**

   a. Did you use application in planning interview? ___ ___

   b. Did you establish rapport? ___ ___

   c. Did you move smoothly into body of interview? ___ ___

Yes   No

2. GETTING INFORMATION

a. Did you ask open-ended questions that elicited information? ___ ___

b. Did you follow through on answers? ___ ___

c. Did you avoid telegraphing desired responses? ___ ___

d. Did you control the interview? ___ ___

e. Did you get applicant to speak freely? ___ ___

f. Did you really listen? ___ ___

g. Did you obtain adequate job factor information? ___ ___

h. Did you obtain adequate intangible factor knowledge? ___ ___

3. GIVING INFORMATION

a. Did you describe job adequately? ___ ___

b. Did you give applicant some background on company? ___ ___

c. Did you "sell" job and company to applicant? ___ ___

d. Did you encourage applicant to ask questions? ___ ___

4. CLOSING THE INTERVIEW

a. Did you control when interview closed? ___ ___

	Yes	No

b. (if applicant was to be rejected)
Did you handle rejection diplomatically? ___ ___

c. (if applicant was to be considered further)
Did you inform applicant of next step in procedure? ___ ___

d. Did you leave applicant with good impression of firm? ___ ___

e. Did you make appropriate notes after applicant left? ___ ___

HOW GOOD AN
EMPLOYMENT INTERVIEWER
ARE YOU?

The following quiz is designed to help you review some of
the major points covered in Part III. You may also want
other managers and subordinates involved in the interviewing process to take the quiz so that you can evaluate their
knowledge and understanding of the interviewing and selection process:

	True	False
1. The first step in filling a job is getting an idea of the job market for the particular skill.	____	____
2. A well-written résumé is as good a source of information as a completed application form.	____	____

		True	False

3. Frequent job changes do not necessarily mean that the applicant is unstable.   ____   ____

4. The first thing a good interviewer does in an interview is to establish rapport with the applicant.   ____   ____

5. The correct way to greet applicants is to have your secretary bring them to your office as soon as they arrive.   ____   ____

6. Even when detailed information on specific areas is required, questions should be open-ended.   ____   ____

7. In nondirective interviewing, the interviewer obtains information by first asking an open-ended question and then remaining silent or giving only a word or gesture to encourage the applicant to continue to talk.   ____   ____

8. The best way to help an applicant to get over initial nervousness is to get down to business as quickly as possible.   ____   ____

9. A good way to obtain information on education and experience is the six basic questions, "What," "When," "Where," "Who," "Why," and "How."   ____   ____

	True	False

10. When prior experience does not reflect managerial ability, creativity or other talents, you can look for them in outside activities. _____ _____

11. While "selling" the company to an applicant may be important, exaggerations can create serious problems. _____ _____

12. Discussing negative aspects of your company is a mistake, since it may discourage a potentially valuable person from accepting the job. _____ _____

13. Salary should not be discussed until the hiring interview. _____ _____

14. Never take notes during an interview because it may distract or intimidate the applicant. _____ _____

15. Skillful interviewers evaluate only those factors that relate to the job that is open and possibly to jobs the current position may lead to. _____ _____

16. The "halo" and "pitchfork" effects refer to the applicant's perception of the interview. _____ _____

17. "Telegraphing" describes an interviewing mistake. _____ _____

		True	False
18.	One way to make sure that you stay alert during an interview is to concentrate on the applicant's facial expressions and other nonverbal behavior.	_____	_____
19.	The first clue that your mind is beginning to wander is when you begin to hear sounds rather than ideas coming from the speaker.	_____	_____
20.	Talking too much is a sign of inexperience or incompetence in an applicant.	_____	_____
21.	Belligerence may hide a real talent for handling authority and demonstrate a "no nonsense" approach to business.	_____	_____
22.	The sequential interview has the advantage of eliminating unqualified people before they take up valuable time from managers.	_____	_____
23.	The serialized interview requires that at least two interviewers must concur before an applicant can be rejected.	_____	_____
24.	The panel interview saves time, but may intimidate applicants.	_____	_____
25.	Job offers should have a reasonable deadline for a decision.	_____	_____

ANSWERS:

1. *False*. The first step in filling a position is a job analysis which comprises the job description, a detailed summary of the duties, responsibilities and other job factors, and the job specifications, the skills and aptitudes needed to perform the job. Availability becomes a factor when determining the salary.

2. *False*. While a résumé may supplement an application, it cannot replace it. An application asks for information the company needs to have. A résumé gives only that information the applicant wants known. Applicants who attempt to submit résumés in place of the completed application should be told that they *must* complete the form.

3. *True*. Instability may be indicated, but the interviewer should find out the reasons for the changes during the job interview. A previous employer's business reversal, another's decision to leave or enter a specific field could account for the frequent moves.

4. *True*. The more relaxed the applicant, the more information he will give. An open, communicative candidate is also easier to evaluate in terms of personal characteristics.

5. *False*. The interviewer should go out and greet the applicant—warmly, enthusiastically and by name. Having a secretary bring the candidate into the interviewer's office where the interviewer sits behind a desk reading the applicant's résumé or application can be very intimidating and will make it difficult to establish rapport.

6. *True*. The descriptive response elicited by an open-ended question will include specific information. The question that requires only a yes or no answer, however, will not get a broad, informative response. Moreover, open-ended questions can be followed by more specific ones. *Example*: Open-ended question—"Tell me about your supervisory responsibilities." Narrow-focus question— "How many people did you supervise?"

7. *True*. Encouraging interviewees to say what is on their minds rather than having them answer a lot of questions may reveal information that the interviewer might never have thought to ask about.

8. *False*. Bland, noncontroversial questions about the weather or the applicant's trip to the interview are the best way to start an interview.

9. *True*. Elaborated, these questions are: "What skills were needed to accomplish the task?" "When did you do this kind of work?" "Where were these skills applicable?" "Who was responsible?" "Why did you make that decision?" "How did you solve this problem?"

10. *True*. The applicant's experience may not show an ability because a previous job, or previous employer, gave no opportunity to develop it. Therefore, you should inquire about talents the candidate may have used in educational, civic, religious, trade or professional association activities. Such abilities, when directed toward work, could make an applicant with acceptable business experience an outstanding employee.

11. *True.* Nothing creates greater bitterness than giving false hope. The employer who creates it may find that an exciting prospect has become an embittered resentful employee.

12. *False.* They'll find out about the shortcomings sooner or later, and the later they find out, the greater the resentment will be. Negative information can, however, be carefully phrased. *Example*: "We've had two bad years, but we expect to do well this year."

13. *False.* Although the specific offer is not made until the hiring interview, general discussions about salary should take place well before then.

14. *False.* Taking notes helps you structure the interview, keep track of subjects you want to know more about (without interrupting the applicant) and remember the applicant after the interview is over. However, note taking should be done judiciously, since writing constantly interferes with both the interviewer's and interviewee's concentration.

15. *True.* For example, a mechanical engineer does not need to be gregarious or assertive and a salesperson may not need to have a gift for finance.

16. *False.* The "halo" refers to an *interviewer's* tendency to project one outstanding ability in an applicant to all areas. Conversely, the "pitchfork" effect is the tendency to project a single shortcoming to general incompetence.

17. *True.* It refers to rhetorical questions which indicate to the applicant the answer that the interviewer wants to hear. For example: "Don't you think that getting along

with subordinates is absolutely critical to good management?"

18. *True*. Experienced interviewers know that it takes an *overt effort* to listen for extended periods of time. Concentrating on nonverbal behavior is a good way to maintain a long span of attention.

19. *True*. Experienced interviewers can spot this in themselves almost immediately. Learning to recognize loss of attention early is an important part of becoming a good interviewer.

20. *False*. Some people simply express their anxiety by talking a lot and this mannerism may hide real ability. You may need to interrupt frequently to ask specific questions. In some instances, however, applicants who are not competent may try to hide their unsuitability by telling endless stories.

21. *False*. Applicants who try to put the interviewer on the defensive or force an argument should not be hired.

22. *True*. Lower-ranking persons in the company can screen out unqualified people early.

23. *True*. Personnel or an administrative assistant screens out the obviously unqualified according to specific guidelines. Those remaining are interviewed by two or more company representatives.

24. *True*. Therefore, when a group of executives is going to interview an applicant in a conference setting—i.e., a panel interview—the applicant should be briefed in advance about who will be on the panel and what its purpose is.

25. *True.* Otherwise, an applicant who has personal reservations or offers from other companies may stall indefinitely.

How to Score Yourself:

25 correct answers—a superior knowledge of interviewing and selection
22–24 correct—excellent
19–21 correct—good
16–18 correct—average
Below 16—poor

INDEX